"Victor Avila is a true patriot and journey through the lens of an immigration officer and the challenges and struggles they face at our southern border. Readers will be humbled by the sacrifices Victor and Jamie Zapata made to protect this country."

-**Congressman Michael McCaul**,
former Chairman of the House Homeland Security

"Former ICE Special Agent Victor Avila's story of survival and courage is a harrowing must read. His dedication to obtaining justice for his partner, Jaime Zapata, who was murdered just inches away while on assignment in Mexico, is honorable and a reflection of his character. The government coverup of what happened and their retaliation against him for telling the truth is unforgivable. You won't be able to put this book down."

-**Katie Pavlich**, Townhall Editor,
Fox News contributor and Best-selling author

"Long after police identified the Mexican cartel hit men who attacked Special Agent Victor Avila and his partner, Jaime Zapata, in 2011-the mystery lingered as to why their supervisors sent them, unprotected, on what was virtually a suicide mission. In Agent Under Fire, Avila deconstructs the nightmare that took his partner's life and robbed him of his health and career, and digs into the larger questions about the complicated U.S. Mexico relationship, drugs, and illegal immigration."

-**Sharyl Attkisson**,
Full Measure Managing Editor,
Investigative Reporter and author

"Avila puts us next to him on the pavement of Mexico's Highway 57; staring evil in the eye, glass shattering, lead flying, shell casing tumbling through the air, the blood of two federal agents spilled by a vicious drug cartel."

-**Jay Dobyns**, Federal Agent (ret.),
New York Times Bestselling Author of No Angel

"Victor Avila is a true American hero. His story is a must read for anyone who wants to know the truth about the risks and battles on the US/Mexican border. After being attacked by drug cartels, fighting for his life and being abandoned by his own government, Victor's love of country remains intact and is an inspiration for all."

-**Dr. Mark Young**,
Entrepreneur and Co-Host of Blunt Force Truth

"The story of Victor Avila and Jaime Zapata may possibly be the most riveting, yet covered up tragedy in recent history. Yet, few Americans have ever heard of what should be known as 'the Mexican Benghazi.' The implication of Avila's accusation is terrifying and reverberates across those very government agencies to this very day. Avila's story is so important because if this cover-up is allowed to continue, other patriotic federal agents serving in volatile theaters will remain at risk, the lives relegated to that of pawns in a chess game of political correctness."

-**Daniel Horowitz**,
Senior Editor-Conservative Review

AGENT
UNDER FIRE

AGENT UNDER FIRE

A Murder And A Manifesto

VICTOR AVILA

LIBERTY HILL PRESS

Liberty Hill Press
2301 Lucien Way #415
Maitland, FL 32751
407.339.4217
www.libertyhillpublishing.com

© 2020 by Victor Avila

Edited by Xulon Press

Printed in the United States of America.

Paperback ISBN-13: 978-1-6322-1529-1
Dust Jacket ISBN-13: 978-1-6322-1530-7
Ebook ISBN-13: 978-1-6322-1531-4

For my wife Claudia
and children, Sofia and Victor Emilio.

TABLE OF CONTENTS

PROLOGUE

I was alive! But I couldn't trust anyone – or I might not stay that way for long.

The Zetas Cartel didn't leave survivors behind. Everyone knew that. With no way to tell who might be on their payroll, I frantically searched each face—police and hospital personnel alike—for any telltale sign of deceit or conspiracy. I had survived the attack on Highway 57, but the Zetas would pull out all the stops to finish the job. I might have made it to the hospital, but I wasn't safe. Not yet.

A nurse approached with scissors, and I braced for a possible attack — until she began cutting off my blood-stained clothes. I clutched my backpack between my legs, unwilling to relinquish it for even a moment, and estimated how long it would take to unzip the bag and grab one of the guns stashed inside.

"I'm going to give you something for the pain," said a man in a white coat.

"No! No medication!" I yelled.

If the doctor was in league with the cartel, medication could be the weapon used to kill me. My adrenaline still surged, and I had yet to feel any pain though I bled from my side, my leg, and too many other places to count. I had used my belt as a makeshift tourniquet, but my leg had swollen to the size of a melon. Pain would surely come later, but I couldn't afford to have my senses dulled. Not until I knew who could be trusted.

I refused to surrender my cell phone and stayed on the line with the federal police while doctors and nurses worked on my wounds. The head of the *federales* was a friend and promised to send someone I could trust. But with corruption running deep in the Mexican police force, it could take hours for officers to be vetted and dispatched to the hospital. In the meantime, I had my wits ... and my backpack.

Where was Jaime? I hadn't seen my partner since the EMTs loaded him into the helicopter. Touching his hand, I had found it growing cold, but whether from loss of blood or ... I didn't want to think the words.

We should never have been on Highway 57. Incidents of ambushes and murders by drug cartels were all-too frequent. Warnings had been issued by the United States embassy stating unequivocally that the stretch of road was too dangerous and was to be avoided. Even special agents traveling in heavily armored SUVs were subject to attack.

Despite the no-travel edict from higher up, my partner Jaime and I were charged with transporting equipment along that unsafe road. After driving to Monterrey to pick up what was needed, we would return to Mexico City by the end of the day. The task had nothing to do with any of the twenty or so cases I currently handled. Operation Pacific Rim wasn't my case—another point of debate. Why weren't the agents assigned to the case given the job? Moving the gear by diplomatic pouch made the most sense. What made the directive even more suspicious was that Agent Zapata and I were refused the traditional precautionary police escort for our mission.

I argued with my supervisors, who scoffed at my fears that the road was unsafe, and insisted that Jaime and I make the drive. Later on, during an internal investigation, they would lie, and insist that they had offered to send someone else on the ill-fated mission, but I had turned them down.

Now I lay in the hospital, covered in blood—both mine and Jaime's—uncertain about the fate of my partner and fearing for my life. Even with guards outfitted in SWAT gear stationed at every entry point and the hospital declared a safe zone, I kept my eyes open.

I was transported to the third floor for increased security. Suddenly, the reverberation of whirring helicopter blades drowned out every other sound. Windows rattled and the building trembled, as a Blackhawk landed in the green area next to the hospital. A few moments later, an officer—second in command of the entire Mexican federal police—entered my room. I recognized him. And he wasn't to be trusted.

Chapter One

BORN IN THE USA

I've never thought of myself as a Mexican. I'm a Mexican-American, with the emphasis on the American part. That doesn't mean I don't love Mexico. I do!

I love Mexico even though I nearly died there, in a barrage of automatic weapons fire. I love her at the same time I grieve over what the bloodthirsty drug cartels and corrupt authorities have done to her. I would give anything to see her people set free from the poverty, fear and misery that grips them.

I have seen many things in Mexico that I wish I had never seen. Like headless bodies hanging upside down from a bridge in the once-gentle Ciudad Juarez — victims of one of Mexico's many brutal drug cartels. I've seen corpses of people who were skinned alive, an unbelievably vicious and painful way to die. I've watched a backhoe pull body after body from a mass burial site just outside the city. I could go on, but even though I've been in law enforcement for years, it makes me sick to my stomach to even think about it. I have come to believe there is no limit to human depravity.

But I'm getting ahead of my story. I was talking about my Mexican heritage. My parents were born in the state of Chihuahua, and I have many cousins in the capital city, which is also named Chihuahua. Ciudad Juarez, which sits across the Rio Grande from El Paso, is the largest city in the state. My mother and father came to the United States – legally – several years before my twin sister, Magdalena, and I were born in El Paso, Texas, in 1972.

I've always been proud to be an American. I'll never forget how my father beamed with joy when he became an American citizen in 1980, or how my mother wept when she became a citizen about ten years later. To this day it fills me with pride to think that I was born here! I am so grateful my parents had the mindset to leave everything behind and come here in the 1960s in search of the American dream.

If I was ever forced to choose between Mexico and the United States, there would be no doubt in my mind. I'd choose the United States every time. I've been a patriot ever since I took my first few steps some 47 years ago. I am convinced this is the greatest country in the world.

My dad, who is also named Victor, served as a police officer for a while in Mexico, and I heard a lot of stories about his wild adventures down there. He was something of a rarity in the Mexico of that time – an honest cop. That may sound harsh. But my dad told me a lot of stories about the corruption he encountered. In fact, that was the main reason he left Mexico for the United States. It's a hard enough job to be fighting criminals all the time, but when you're not sure which of your fellow officers is really on your side, that makes it next to impossible.

I know there are many fine and loyal law enforcement officers in Mexico today. Many of them have put their lives on the line – and have lost their lives – fighting the vicious, heavily armed drug cartels. But most of the stories my father told me about his time wearing a badge didn't do anything to make me want to follow in his footsteps. My parents tell me now that I talked about being a policeman from the time I was a very small boy. I'm sure that's not unusual. Most boys want to be cops or firemen when they grow up, and the dream never faded for me.

By the time I was born, my dad was working as a contractor. His uncles were all in construction, taught him the trade, and that's what he did until he retired.

———

Another thing about my parents is that they came from totally opposite backgrounds. My dad was an only child who grew up with his mother after she divorced my grandfather, who, like my father, served as a law enforcement officer in Chihuahua and Ciudad Juarez. My dad was a free-spirited young man who liked to socialize. At one point when he was a child, my dad went to a school in El Paso, which is where he learned to speak English.

My mom, Magdalena, like my sister, was one of five girls who grew up in a stable two-parent home. They all lived in a beautiful house with a courtyard in the middle, where everyone followed the rules, and Sunday morning mass was never missed. Her father made beautiful hand-stitched saddles that were of the finest quality. Because of their backgrounds, my parents are total opposites. But somehow, they've made it work for over 50 years.

In fact, they married each other three times. Once in Mexico, once in California and once in Texas. I think they wanted to make sure they were married wherever they are.

I also have two sisters, including my twin, who is an attorney in Arlington, Texas, and Janette, who was born in California in 1968. Janette is an accomplished professional who earned her high school diploma in three years – and then went straight to work as a property manager, something she's had great success with for over 30 years.

My parents are great, fun, people, and I have many happy memories of my childhood. My mom and dad are both extremely social. They have always had plenty of friends and hosted lots of parties at our house. Everyone had a good time dancing and the atmosphere was always happy. My parents worked hard, and people love and respect them. This is attested by the fact that they have 29 godchildren. That's a lot of christenings and first com-munions. My wife, Claudia, and I now have nine godchildren of our own.

My mom and dad have always encouraged my sisters and me to work hard and always do our best. They weren't overbearing or unreasonable in their expectations. They just wanted us to succeed in life and to have a plan rather than just drifting along wherever life took us.

Largely as a result of the ambition they instilled in me, I started working when I was fifteen, helping my dad in his construction business, doing whatever he needed me to do. When I turned sixteen and was old enough to get my driver's license, I started driving a truck for him, and was in charge of making sure all the vehicles were well maintained and in good working order. I also spent some time sorting mail and handling other jobs at our local post office and worked as a stock boy at a grocery store. Between school, karate and working, I put in some very long days and weeks, but it taught me how to juggle a number of different projects at once, a skill I would desperately need years later as an ICE Special Agent.

I was still in junior high school when my dad started making suggestions about what I should do after I graduated from high school. "I know you're interested in cars. Maybe you should become a mechanic?"

"But Dad. . ."

"Have you thought about it? You know, it will be here before you know it."

"Yes, Dad, I *have* thought about it. And I'm going to go to college."

"College?"

"Yes. Right here at UTEP."

He hadn't even thought of that. But he and my mom were thrilled to think that I would be among the first in my family to pursue a university degree. And when they discovered that Magdalena also had her sights set on college, they were so proud.

———

It was also in my teen years that I had the experience that cemented my desire to go into law enforcement: I had the privilege of becoming a Police Explorer. That meant I got my own uniform, was able to go on ride-alongs with members of the El Paso Police Department and learn about police work from the inside. There were plenty of exciting times. But I also learned that a policeman's job can be excruciatingly boring! There are so many times when you're just driving around, waiting for something to happen. And then there are the mountains of paperwork! Because of that, I had a fairly realistic view of what it means to work in law enforcement. I knew better than to think that a policeman's life was one thrill upon another.

I also learned that police officers are ordinary people, trying to do the best job they can. I was brought up to respect authority, and particularly if that authority was represented by a uniform. But because of that, I was also somewhat intimidated by men and women in uniform. Sometimes, respect crossed the line into fear. But when I saw that cops are real people, my fear completely dissipated.

————

When I look back on my childhood, I have many happy memories of times spent in our church, Corpus Christi, which was built in 1979. It wasn't your typical church by any means, and I think that's one of the things that made it so special. The church building actually looked like a home, and the Masses were held in the garage. Sometimes, Sunday Mass was moved to other homes in the neighborhood, including ours. I'll always remember what a thrill it was to have Sunday Mass at our house. That unique congregation was a vital part of our community, and I have terrific memories of parties, festivals, and spending time learning about God's love. Magdalena's Quinceanera was held there on her 15th birthday, a great event in the life of every Hispanic girl. And as her brother, I was a member of her court of honor.

It was in that church that I found the faith that has sustained me during the most difficult times of my life.

I also learned a lot about the importance of faith from my dad. Even though he never went to church with us, he had more faith than just about anyone I've ever met. He lived close to God, prayed every day, and lived out his faith in every circumstance. But for some reason, church wasn't for him. I learned from him not to put my faith in the "church box" and leave it there. He believed that faith was for every day of the week — not just Sunday.

5

The only time things got a bit "bumpy" in our family was on Friday nights. That was the night my dad went out drinking with his friends. My mother didn't like it, but it was time Dad had set aside for himself and he wasn't about to give it up. I knew he went out to drink, but like everything else, he was responsible about it. I never saw him drunk or even tipsy that I can remember. My mom just wanted him to be at home with his family. And, as the years went by, he stayed home Friday more and more, until those nights out with the boys became a thing of the past.

I have been asked if I ever experienced racism when I was a boy growing up in El Paso, and the answer is no. Most of the other children in my school were of Hispanic origin, just like me, as were most of the people who lived in my neighborhood.

Because I was of Mexican heritage, I always felt that I had to work hard to prove myself. I had a lot of white friends, and when I was with them, I felt the need to show that I was just as good as they were. I spoke excellent English. I worked hard to get good grades in school. I wanted to show them that there wasn't anything they could do that I couldn't do. When I was with my Hispanic friends, I wanted them to know that I was as much of a Mexican as they were, so I spoke the slang, dropped a few Spanish words into my conversation from time to time, etc.

At home, my dad always insisted that his children speak English. He would remind us that our future was in the United States, and that we must learn to speak the language of the country that would give us so many opportunities. My father never said a bad word about his native Mexico. But he was full of admiration for the United States.

———

I don't want to give the impression that my childhood was always a happy place where the sun was shining down on me. I had some difficult times during my first few years of elementary school because I was so small and fragile. I was underweight, short for my age, and I had heart murmurs which kept me from participating in physical activities with the other boys and girls.

My parents were trying hard to fix me, but nothing worked. I drank goat milk until I felt like I was about to sprout horns on the top of my head.

"It's full of vitamins," my mother said. But it didn't help me.

I also took a variety of tonics and supplements, but they didn't seem to help either.

Third grade was the worst year for me. Most of the time, when the other kids went to P.E., or out to play at recess, I stayed in the classroom with my teacher. I felt humiliated and had almost no self-confidence. Luckily for me, my teacher was a caring woman who wanted to make our time together worthwhile. When the other kids were out running and playing, she drilled me on my vocabulary words and I became an excellent speller. That gained me some much-needed self-esteem and respect. I was always one of the last kids standing during a class spelling bee. She also worked hard with me on math. With her help, I went from being an average student to one of the best in the class. She also put me in charge of the garden we were growing, and to this day I love working in my garden. I enjoy being surrounded by plants and flowers of all types.

I was growing by leaps and bounds intellectually, but not physically. I just couldn't seem to catch up with the other kids, and I began to think that my dream of being in law enforcement could never come true. How could a kid like me grow up to be a big, strong cop? Then one day, something marvelous came into my life.

Karate!

I was 11-years-old when my dad took me to a karate class for the first time. There were all these kids – some smaller than me – wearing cool-looking white uniforms, huffing and puffing as they kicked and fought their way around the room.

"You think you can do this?" my dad asked.

"Of course, I can," I replied.

And I wasn't lying. For some reason, I knew karate was going to change my life. And it did!

When the class was over, Dad introduced me to the Sensei (or instructor), and told him I wanted to be a part of his group. He bowed and welcomed me politely. He seemed happy to meet me, although I know I was small and skinny and didn't look like much of a prospect. Looking back on it now, I realize that every child needs to find something he's good at. Mine was karate.

I had a knack for it right away, and the Sensei, whose name was Ray, often called me to the front to show the other kids the various moves he was talking about. I could kick. Thrust. Swing those nunchucks, and I was hard to beat when it came to Tiger wrestling. I moved quickly up the ranks, earning my white, blue, brown and then black belts. I kept going on up through my black belt. My success gave me confidence in other areas of my life. I worked out hard and it showed.

Ray, who had come to the United States from Jamaica, and went on to become a DEA agent, became a very important influence in my life. He was one of the most positive people I've ever known, and became something of a second dad to me. In fact, his daughter April is now my sister-in-law, having married Claudia's brother, Jaime.

Ray was tough, but fair, and never belittled any of us or talked down to us. I remember that he would often have us line up and hold our arms out, and then he would check our fingernails to make sure they were neatly trimmed. He wanted us all to be proud of who we were, and a part of that pride would be seen in how we took care of our bodies.

Over time, I developed a solid six-pack, and I knew that I could take care of myself if anyone tried to pick on me. I never started a fight, but I never backed away from one either. One of the important things karate gave me was an understanding of personal honor and sportsmanship. The power of karate is cloaked by gentleness and kindness. It gave me a solid foundation for my life and career.

Karate was an important part of my life every day for 15 years. I couldn't get enough of it. Then other things came into my life that left little room for it. Things like getting married, starting a career and raising a family. Still, I love karate and will always appreciate how it transformed my life.

———

Then, a month or so before the end of my junior year of high school, my life changed again. That's when I met Claudia, the girl I was going to marry.

She just showed up in school one day, and I was shocked that I hadn't noticed her before.

I immediately asked one of my buddies if he knew who she was, but he had no idea. I knew that I had never seen her before, because if I had, I would have remembered.

"Oh, man," my friend teased me, "Victor's in love!" He tried to punch me on the arm, but I danced out of his way.

"I'm not in love," I protested. "She's just interesting."

That she was. First, she was beautiful, with lovely light-brown hair framing her perfect face. I was also intrigued by the fact that she wore a bright red pair of glasses. Those frames were so cool, and they made her stand out from the rest. I also liked the way she looked in her long, flowing prairie dress. I think they might have called them "granny dresses" back in the 70's, but she didn't look anything like a granny to me. She had her own unique style, and that was one of the things that appealed to me, although I did tease her later on about looking like she had stepped right off the TV show, *Little House on the Prairie*.

Like me, Claudia was born in El Paso, although her parents were both born in Mexico. And in the 1980s, when the devaluation of the peso caused prices to plummet in Mexico, her family bought a house on the other side of the Rio Grande River, in Ciudad Juarez. In those days, because the dollar was so strong against the peso, some people on the Mexican side of the river were making mortgage payments of only a few dollars a month. Still, Claudia had never gone to school in Mexico. She had come across the Santa Fe Street Bridge – also known as the Paso Del Norte Bridge – and went to school in El Paso. Until recently, she had been attending a Catholic all-girls school, Father Yermo High School.

What I didn't know was that her family had decided to move back into the United States, and they were looking to buy a house in my neighborhood. That meant she had transferred to my high school, Del Valle, which was good news for me.

I saw her in school a few more times after that, but never had a chance to talk to her. Or, maybe I was trying to get up enough nerve to say hello. I'm not really sure which it was.

At the time, I was still very much involved in karate, and some of my friends and I were often asked to perform at halftimes of games, intermissions of plays, etc. We broke blocks of wood with our bare hands, shattered bricks by kicking them with our bare feet – and our classmates seemed to love it. A few weeks after I first spotted Claudia, we were asked to perform at the intermission of a dance recital on Friday night. When the recital was over, several of us went to a nearby pizza parlor.

I was standing in line, waiting for my pizza, when somebody tapped me on the shoulder.

I turned around and found myself looking into a luminous pair of big hazel eyes that were looking back at me through a pair of bright red classes.

"I know you," she said. "I've seen you do karate. You're really good."

At least, I think that's what she said. To be honest, I didn't hear anything after, "I know you." I couldn't believe that she was talking to me.

"I'm Claudia," she smiled.

"Victor," I smiled back and extended my hand. I could tell you that was the beginning of a beautiful love story and that we all lived "happily ever after," — and eventually we did — but there were a few twists and turns in the road before we got there.

It wasn't until several weeks later that we had our first date. We went bowling with a friend of mine and Claudia's sister, Sandra. I had a great time talking to her, and the more I got to know her, the more I liked her. Her parents were genteel people who carried themselves with an old-world dignity and obviously cared a great deal about their daughter. They weren't about to let her go out on a date with just anybody. Before we left the house on our date that night, they wanted to find out who I was.

That wasn't a problem for me. I had always been respectful to my elders. I was never a smart-mouth or a show-off. Claudia's mom and dad liked me, and we went out to enjoy our time together.

After that, we dated off and on for a while, although we never went steady or anything like that. We liked each other, but we were young and not ready to commit to anything. It didn't take long for me to see Claudia's innate intelligence and ability. She had big plans for the future and I knew she could do anything she put her mind to.

She was my date for my senior prom that year, and I will never forget how stunning she looked in her beautiful white party dress with black polka dots. Still, I let her get away.

I'm not going to tell you that I knew from the moment I saw Claudia that God wanted us to be together – but it certainly seems to me now that He did. Every time we seemed about to go our separate ways, he brought us back together. As an example of that, I think of what happened during the summer after our junior year in high school. One day, after not talking to Claudia for a few weeks, I decided to give her a call.

She seemed a bit breathless when she answered the phone.

"Your timing is great," she said. "We were just walking out the door."

"Walking out the door?" I repeated. "Where are you going?"

"We've moving," she said.

"Moving? Now?"

"That's right."

I hadn't known it, but Claudia and her family had sold their house and were moving across town. They were just about to walk out and lock the door behind them. If that had happened, I might never have seen her again. But because I called when I did, she gave me her new phone number and we were able to keep in touch.

Like most of my friends in El Paso, we all wound up going to college at the University of Texas at El Paso (UTEP). I knew she was there, but I never saw her. That's not surprising because UTEP has more than 25,000 students and is spread out over 421 acres. I thought about her from time to time, of course, but I figured that boat had sailed and there was nothing I could do about it.

Then one day, as I was heading home after a day of classes, I saw a pretty young woman standing in a parking lot, in front of her car with the hood up. She was peering under the hood in a way that prevented me from seeing her face, but I decided to stop and see if I could help.

I pulled into the parking space next to her car, waving and smiling to let her know my intentions were good.

I rolled down the passenger side window and called out, "Can I give you a hand?"

She stood up straight and looked at me, and I saw those same beautiful hazel eyes I knew so well, minus the glasses with the red frames which, I suppose, had been retired.

"Claudia!"

"Victor!"

We both laughed when we saw each other, but Claudia's smile only lasted a few seconds. She was too upset about her car to keep smiling.

"What's the matter with it?" I asked.

"Oh, it's been on its last legs for a long time," she said. "I think the end has finally come."

"Well, what can I do to help?"

She looked at her watch and frowned.

"I'm going to be late for work. Can you give me a ride?"

"Sure. But what are you going to do about your car?"

"I don't know. I'll see if my dad can get it towed."

I helped her gather her books and her purse, she climbed into the passenger side of my car, and I took her home.

As we drove out, I told her it was really good to see her and asked what was going on in her life. Although I didn't say anything about it, it felt pretty good to have her sitting beside me in my car. She told me she had a boyfriend, and that they had been dating for a couple of months. I felt jealous, even though I had no right to feel that way.

"How about you?" she asked. "Oh, I have one, too. I mean, not a boyfriend, but. . ."

"I got it," she laughed.

Hmmm. Why did she ask me if I was dating someone? Could it be that she was jealous, too? It was a funny thing about my relationship with Claudia. I never made any kind of commitment to her, yet I always got jealous when she went out with other guys.

A few weeks after her car broke down, my girlfriend and I broke up, so I called Claudia to see what was going on with her. Surprise! She and her boyfriend had decided to go their separate ways. I immediately asked her out, she said yes, and from that time on we were together. But it's not like we rushed to the altar. We dated seven years before we got married. By that time, both sets of parents were getting anxious, and Claudia and I received quite a few hints – some subtle and others not-so subtle.

They seemed to know we were made for each other before we did – and didn't want us to break up again. They really didn't need to worry about it, because we had both come to the same realization. It seemed to me that fate was working to keep us together. The breakdown of her car was one example of this.

We knew we loved each other, but we wanted to get through college before we married, and we also wanted to buy a home. So, we bought a brand-new house about a year before our wedding. And we were able to move in the day of our wedding. We felt like we were living in a fairy tale.

By this time, Claudia was working as an investigator for Child Protective Services, looking into suspected cases of child abuse, and I had a job as a parole officer, working for the state of Texas, and we've been an unstoppable team ever since.

Chapter Two

MR. AGENT MAN

For the next year and a half, Claudia and I were very happy in El Paso. We both loved the city and felt quite comfortable there. The only problem was that an increasing amount of drugs were pouring over the border into El Paso, and quite a bit of them stayed there. As a result, the crime rate in our city rose constantly. I also felt frustrated and sad when I heard about growing violence in Juarez. . .but I had no real idea of the evil that was growing just beyond the border.

Like most young couples, Claudia and I were focused on building our home and our family, and we were thrilled beyond measure when, after about a year in El Paso, we received the terrific news that we were going to have a baby. It was so much fun to share the good news with our parents, who were just as excited as we were, and then we threw our energy into getting the nursery ready.

Then, another surprise came. Exactly one week after we discovered Claudia was pregnant, I received a job offer to work for the federal government as a United States Probation Officer in San Antonio. The job represented a big step up in my career. It offered more money, better perks, and more opportunities for advancement. Of course, I felt excited about the new position, but also sad that Claudia and I would have to move out of the house that we loved so much, and distance ourselves from our parents at this critical time. I know it was difficult for Claudia, but she never showed a moment of disappointment, unhappiness or worry.

As I knew would be the case, our move wasn't easy for our parents, especially hers. Generally, Hispanics are extremely family-oriented and tend to stay close to each other. For example, when Claudia, who was an exceptional student, received an acceptance letter from Brown University, her parents forbade her to go.

"You're staying right here where your family is," her mother told her. "I won't have you going halfway across the country."

Some kids would have gone anyway, but Claudia didn't argue. She did as her mother said and enrolled at UTEP.

San Antonio wasn't exactly half the country away from El Paso. The distance was 550 miles to be exact. But that was too far for her mom and dad, who reluctantly let us go, just a few months before their first granddaughter, our daughter Sofia, was born.

Claudia and I went to work finding a renter for our house, packed up a U-Haul and made the trip to San Antonio. Our parents were all standing there, watching as we drove away, waving goodbye, with our moms trying hard not to look like they were going to cry. I know that Claudia and I both drove out of El Paso with lumps in our throats and knots in our stomach. But as soon as we hit the edge of town, we forgot about our sorrow and began to be excited about the adventure that lay ahead. We looked forward to starting our new jobs, getting to know San Antonio, and especially to welcoming our first child into the world. We couldn't wait to see her face, to hold her in our arms and tell her we loved her. It seemed that everything was coming together for us. Child Protective Services had even transferred Claudia's job from El Paso to San Antonio, which meant that she could continue to do what she loved, which eased our transition to the new city.

––––––––

As it turned out, we loved San Antonio. But we weren't there very long.

About seven months after we moved there, my boss called me into her office one day and said, "I just found out there's a job opening in El Paso. Are you interested?"

I didn't know what to say. I didn't want to make it seem like I wasn't totally satisfied in San Antonio.

"I know you're from El Paso," she said. "So I wondered if. . ."

"It's not like I want to go back," I smiled. "But my wife would love it. She really misses her family."

She told me that she appreciated the job I did for her and that she'd hate to see me go. "But I know how important it is for new moms to be close to their mothers. And it sounds like a great opportunity for you."

I called Claudia and, as I expected, she was delighted by the chance to go back home. In fact, she was so delighted that she wanted to go right away. After all, being eight months pregnant, she wanted to get everything set up in El Paso so she could have the baby there. Of course, her parents could barely contain their joy, and mine felt the same way. A few days later, her brother drove up to San Antonio and took her home with him to El Paso.

I had to stay a few weeks longer to wrap up some loose ends in San Antonio and got back to El Paso in late April or early May. Just in time for Sofia's entrance into the world in June – a beautiful girl just like her mother. I can't even begin to explain how I felt when I held her in my arms. I realize that if you're a dad or a mom – you already know.

It seemed that everything was going our way, and we were looking forward to a bright future together. I appreciated El Paso for many reasons, including the fast tempo of my job. I like to keep busy, and believe me, things were always hopping in El Paso. One time, during this period, I attended a training session in Washington, D.C. There were at least 100 probation officers packed into a classroom when the instructor asked, "How many of you have done at least one pre-sentencing report for a judge?"

Ten of us raised our hands.

"How many of you have done more than one?"

Five hands went down.

"Five?"

Two left.

"Ten?"

My arm was the last one raised.

"Twenty?" Still up.

"Thirty?" "Fifty?"

The truth was that I had done hundreds of these reports, and nobody else had done as many as ten. Some of the people in that room thought I was being funny. But that's just how busy it was in El Paso.

Claudia was busy, too. As much as she loved her job with Child Protective Services, she had taken a new job as a sales rep for a pharmaceutical company. The new job offered more flexible hours and seemed tailor-made for a new mom.

But it was very hard work, especially at first when the learning curve was so steep. She was learning about different medications and competitor products, the mechanisms of action, indications, and when they should be prescribed and how they work together. She spent hours at the dining room table sometimes late into the night, with stacks of papers and books in front of her. It was almost like she'd gone back to school to get a degree in pharmacy.

She was determined to know everything she could about the medications she was selling, and, just as I expected, she was exceptionally good at her new job. As I said earlier, I know she'd be great at anything she puts her mind to.

Everything was going along fine for four years, and then I suddenly felt like, "I don't want to do this anymore."

What happened? It was like this. . .

One of the things I had to do, as a part of my job, was put together investigative reports for the district judges. In order to do this, I had to talk to a number of special agents from a variety of law-enforcement agencies, including the FBI, Customs, the Secret Service, and the Immigration and Naturalization Service. I told my friends, "I'm tired of talking to these special agents. I don't want to _hear_ about what they do. I want to _do_ what they do."

A lot of people tried to talk me out of it. In fact, they told me I was crazy! "Do you know how hard it is to get a job as a U.S. probation officer?" And I did know how hard it was. There were thousands of people hoping to land a job like mine. Some people considered it a dream job. You worked Monday through Friday, 9 a.m. to 5 p.m. You wore a suit every day, and didn't have to worry about getting stabbed or shot. After you had done this for 20 years, you could retire with a nice pension. But that wasn't for me. I wanted to be out on the streets making a difference.

So late in 2003, I applied for a job as a special agent for the United States Customs Service. What I didn't know when I applied was that the Department of Homeland Security was being created through a merger of the U.S. Customs Service and the Immigration and Naturalization Service to create ICE (Immigration and Customs Enforcement).

In August of 2004, I was offered a position as a special agent, and left El Paso for the Training Academy in Glynco, Georgia.

———

It was one of the most difficult decisions of my life. The Academy lasted 22 weeks – almost half a year – and I would be halfway across the country from Claudia, who was nearly eight months pregnant with our second child. It was a great opportunity for me, but the timing was lousy. And yet, attending the academy had been my dream for so long. I was torn, but, as usual, my wife insisted that I go.

We went to one of our favorite restaurants to discuss the matter, but she didn't think there was anything to talk about. As usual, she was focused on what the opportunity meant for me. When I started to protest, she didn't want to hear it.

"You have to go," she said. "This is the opportunity you've been waiting for."

Under the table, I reached over and patted her bulging tummy.

"But are you sure you'll be okay without me?"

She laughed and took my hand. "Don't you know me by now?"

And, of course, I did know her. Beautiful. Loving. Kind. And completely confident and self-reliant. Yes, she most certainly could take care of things while I was away.

"But what if something. . .?"

"Nothing will go wrong," Claudia said, answering my question before I even finished asking it. "I want you to go, and that's that."

A few days later, I kissed Claudia goodbye and drove out of El Paso, headed for the East Coast. One of my best friends, Gabriel, went along with me to keep me company on the long trip. Gabriel and another friend named Mike were two of my favorite people. They were both great guys who worked as caseworkers at a halfway house where some of El Paso's worst drug offenders and sex offenders were slowly being reintegrated into society. I got to know Gabriel and Mike when I was a parole officer, and one of them later went into law enforcement. In fact, when I left for the Academy, Mike took my position as a parole officer. He went on to become a Border Patrol Agent and then a DEA Special Agent.

We spent eleven hours on the road that day and were still in Texas at the end of it all. After spending the night in Houston, I stayed on Interstate 10 all the way to Florida, then finally headed an hour north to Glynco and the Academy.

I figured the academy would be crowded, but I was mistaken. At the time, it seemed as if everyone in authority was still trying to figure out how the Customs Service and the Immigration and Naturalization Service were going to fit together.

As it turned out, there were two groups of 24 trainees. One group was training to work for the U.S. Customs Service, and members of the other group were headed into the Secret Service. The first ten weeks was a criminal investigator program that included all of us. After that, the Secret Service group was sent to Maryland while we stayed in Georgia. It was a much smaller group than I expected, and there were other surprises, too.

I had seen photos of the place where we would be staying, and it certainly didn't look like anything to write home about. I was going to be living a very spartan existence. In fact, I had been advised to bring everything I thought I was going to need: Sheets and blankets, towels, cookware, "and if you want a TV or a radio, you'll have to bring that, too." It looked like a college dorm. One of those places where there is one bathroom between two rooms and each room has two beds. And no air conditioning or other "modern" conveniences. Imagine my surprise when, upon my arrival, I was taken to a modern, well-landscaped, freshly painted building. It looked like a brand-new Marriott Hotel, surrounded by old rather run-down dormitories. When you walked through the door, you saw that the place was inviting and beautiful inside. They called it the Taj Mahal, and I could see why. The first ten weeks, I felt like I was living in paradise. I had a nice room with a king bed and my own bathroom, cable TV, air conditioning, which is important in the early fall in Glynco, and everything else I could possibly want.

Then they kicked us out to save money, and into the cheapo, dumpy dorms we went. Talk about going from the penthouse to the basement!

———

Of course, one of the first things I did after getting settled was phone home to check on Claudia. As usual, she told me everything was fine. The baby, Victor Emilio, was due to be delivered by caesarian section on September 16, which is Mexican Independence Day, and our obstetrician saw no reason to believe that date might change. Meanwhile, Claudia was getting lots of help from Sofia, who had just turned four, and couldn't wait to see her brother for the first time – and give him a big hug and a kiss.

Thankfully, the last six weeks of Claudia's pregnancy went according to plan and our son came into the world right on schedule.

I was on the phone with Claudia until the moment she went into surgery. I felt my chest swell with pride knowing how brave she had been thus far. I was glad that her parents were there with her, but brokenhearted that I couldn't be.

"I love you, Babe," I said.

"I know. I love you, too." Somebody said something to her on the other end of the line, I couldn't quite make out what it was, and she said, "Looks like it's time for me to go."

As I hung up the phone, I felt an empty ache in my chest. I felt that I should be with her, even though I knew there wasn't much I could do for her even if I were there. It was all up to God, the doctors, and nurses.

The next time I talked to her was about five hours later, although it felt like a week. "Victor," Claudia said, with great emotion in her voice. "We have a beautiful baby boy!"

Thanks to some help from my friends and instructors at the Academy, I was able to get a quick, surprise flight home the next day, which was a Friday. What a treat that was, getting to tell Claudia and Sofia how much I loved them, and holding my son Victor for the very first time. I got to take them all home from the hospital, spent Saturday with them, and then flew back to the East Coast – and the Academy – early Sunday morning.

––––––––

The trip was way too short – but it put a permanent smile on my face that was noticed for the last several weeks of the Academy. In February, Claudia, Sophia, Victor Emilio, my parents, and my sister Janette honored me by making the trip to Georgia to attend my graduation, which was a very proud occasion for me.

As excited as I was about my graduation, though, I was even more excited about getting home. By this time, I had my dream job waiting for me in El Paso and was anxious to start using everything I had learned during my 22 weeks of training.

Chapter Three

AGENT ON ASSIGNMENT

I called my new supervisor, Kenny Williams, and told him that I'd be driving back to Texas over the weekend and would see him on Monday.

"Let's just plan on you coming in on Tuesday," he said. "Take Monday to do what you need to do – get settled into your house and then we'll see you Tuesday morning."

I was anxious to get started. But I also appreciated having an extra day after driving the 1700 miles from Glynco to El Paso. So I went to work on Tuesday morning, and that's when I got my government vehicle, and what is known as a "battle bag" with gloves, flashlights and similar items, and a duty kit, which has a camera and other investigative tools. I also got what is known as a throwdown badge. It's not your official badge, but it goes around your neck to show anyone your authority when needed.

I was now a full-fledged Special Agent.

Don't misunderstand me. I didn't feel particularly special or otherwise. My gun and my badge were part of the tools I needed to do my job. I've never been interested in overbearing individuals. My desire was to get criminals off the streets – and nothing more.

I was assigned to work with a narcotics conspiracy investigations group, trying to stem the never-ending supply of drugs that were coming into the United States through El Paso.

My first arrest couldn't have been easier. If they were all like this, my job was going to be a piece of cake. But of course, that was far from the truth.

While on a duty call, a large truck had been pulled over by Customs and Border Protection (CBP) Officers as it crossed the port of entry into Texas. The driver looked nervous. And an inspection revealed that the vehicle had a cargo of several thousand pounds of pot.

As he was being hauled off to jail, I stayed behind to go through the vehicle for further evidence.

Suddenly, I heard a chirping noise coming from somewhere under the driver's seat.

I fished around under the seat and pulled out a ringing cell phone.

I hesitated just a moment, and then tapped the screen to answer the call.

"Si?"

"Where are you?" a man asked in Spanish. "We've been waiting for you to call."

I responded that I had run into some heavy traffic, but I was across the border now, and ready to meet them."

Apparently, the fact that I spoke Spanish, without an American accent, convinced them that I was on the up and up.

Without hesitation, they told me that I was to meet them in the parking lot of a nearby Golden Corral restaurant. Did I know where that was?

As a matter of fact, I did. He gave me specific instructions regarding where he and his partner were parked and how I could recognize them, and I told them I'd be there in ten minutes.

After calling my supervisor for backup, I pulled on a pair of jeans and a green polo shirt and climbed behind the wheel of the smuggler's truck. I eased the big truck into gear – actually, "eased" isn't quite accurate — and headed out onto the highway. I wasn't sure what was waiting for me at the Golden Corral and had a tight grip on the steering wheel. By the time I arrived at the Golden Corral restaurant, I was drenched in sweat.

The men I was supposed to meet were waiting right where they said they'd be — but they just sat in their car, waiting for me to come to them. What if they knew I was an officer?

I grabbed my gun, held it down against my pants leg where no one could see it, and climbed out of the truck.

Still no movement on their part. They sat in the front seat of their car with the windows rolled down, as I strolled right up to the driver's side window.

Then, before the driver could react, I thrust my gun through the open window and pressed the barrel against his temple.

"You're under arrest mother fucker!" I shouted. "Get out of the car now!"

Both men immediately did as I asked. They both came out of their vehicle with their hands high in the air, as the rest of my team, who had been hiding nearby, swooped in to frisk and handcuff the two criminals. All in all, it wasn't a bad day for an agent just out of the academy.

———

A few days later, I was in my office when I got a call telling me that a white van was stalled in the middle lane of the interstate, just on the Mexico side of the border.

The driver and his partner had apparently stalled there, and when they did, they jumped out of the truck and ran back into Mexico.

"Okay," I said. "I'm on my way. Don't touch it. Wait until I get there."

Obviously, if the driver and his partner had run away from the scene, there was something they didn't want us to find.

I hopped into my car and was at the border inside of ten minutes.

"Oh, no!" I groaned when I saw what had happened to the abandoned truck. It was now on the American side of the border, pulled off on the side of the road, while a handful of Customs and Border Protection (BCP) officers swarmed all over it.

In my exasperation, I jammed on the brakes, squealed to a stop and ran over to the van. "What are you doing?" I shouted. "Stop it!"

The way they were tearing that truck apart, I knew they were destroying all the evidence. Fingerprints? Good luck with that. Hairs from the driver or fibers from his clothing? No such luck.

"Why didn't you leave this vehicle where it was?" I asked, speaking to no one in particular.

"It was blocking traffic," someone said. "People were getting upset!"

"This is a criminal investigation," I told them. "Not a routine traffic stop." As I walked over to the van, the smell of marijuana almost knocked me over! I didn't need any drug-sniffing dogs on this one. You could have smelled this thing coming down the freeway.

What I saw made me gasp with a bit of grudging admiration. The back of this van had been completely hollowed out and was completely filled with marijuana bricks –1600 of them — worth several hundred dollars each. Whoever had filled this vehicle with pot was an artist. He or she had stacked the bricks in such a way that it would be impossible to add even a few more ounces. The bricks extended under the driver's seat and filled most of the cab. There was no room for a passenger. Another amazing thing was that no attempt had been made to hide the pot. It was right there in plain sight.

After inspecting the truck itself, my next order of business was to view the video tape from the port of entry, to find out what exactly had happened to the truck.

There was the truck, slowing down as it rolled toward the border. The view was so clear I could see the panicked expression on the driver's face.

Fifty yards or so from the border, the truck came to a complete stop.

The driver and his partner, both wearing jeans, T-shirts and tennis shoes, jumped out of the truck, ran around to the front and opened the hood. They stood staring at the engine for perhaps 10 or 15 seconds, puzzled looks on their faces – and then took off running back into Mexico.

They stopped, stared at each other for a moment, and then took off running — back into Mexico.

For them, there couldn't have been a worse time for the truck to break down. But I wondered... how in the world did those guys think they were going to get that load of pot across the border? After all, they hadn't even tried to hide it.

The only plausible answer was not something I wanted to think about: We had a crooked CBP officer.

I had seen this before. The way it worked was that the officer would find out what lane she was going to be assigned to at a particular time and pass the word along to the drug cartel. Then, when the truck or trucks came through, the agent would wave them on through the checkpoint, and get paid a significant amount of cash for each one.

That was apparently what was supposed to happen in this case. Now we had to find out who on our team was working for the smugglers.

We had learned by this time that, for some reason, drug smugglers often come through the border in groups of three. A further review of the film showed that this seemed to be the case here. There were two other vans that seemed to be traveling with the one that had been left on the Interstate. Both of them had passed through the checkpoint without hesitation. They had come to what is known as a California stop – a rolling stop – when they reached the checkpoint. The officer didn't even come out of her booth to see if there was anything suspicious. Instead, she just waved them on through.

We now had a suspect, but we still had to catch her in the act.

In order to do this, we couldn't let on that we suspected her. We just had to keep a very close eye on her. We even sent a crew in during the middle of the night, when she wasn't on duty, of course, and put several more cameras into a small closet area to make sure we were watching her at all times. Those cameras were powerful, with very high resolution. They were so good that we could clearly see people going into a grocery store on the Mexico side of the checkpoint.

Then, on a Saturday night, maybe a week and a half after we began surveilling her, she received a phone call that caused her to burst into tears. "I've got to go!" she shouted, running to her boss. "They just killed my boyfriend! They killed my boyfriend!"

"Well go!" he urged her in the direction of her car, "Go!"

We watched as she ran out to the parking lot, jumped into her car and burned rubber as she headed across the border. Several vehicles, mostly pickup trucks, were waiting to escort her into the city of Juarez.

"Man, she's got a lot of protection over there," someone said. It was obvious that she had a lot of friends in Juarez.

As soon as she left, we made some phone calls to find out who had been murdered in Juarez that night. On a Saturday night, you could usually plan on several homicides in a city like Juarez – but it turned out that there had been just one killing in Juarez on this particular night, and the victim was a known drug dealer. We now knew beyond any doubt that we had our woman. All we had to do was catch her in the act.

Our opportunity came a few nights later, when she was back on duty. Unfortunately, I wasn't on call that particular night.

Once again, this time, three vans were seen heading toward the border in close proximity to each other. Once again, the agent waved them on through, without even gesturing for them to stop.

This time, the Border Patrol was waiting and ready. The officers had been sitting in their car, keeping close watch on the suspect. Now they came rushing to the scene with lights flashing and sirens screaming.

The first van made it through the border, but the driver knew right away that he wasn't going to get much further.

He swerved around, trying to flip a U and head back into Mexico.

Instead, he lost control, went off the road and slammed into a retaining wall.

Meanwhile, other agents swarmed in to arrest the smugglers and the crooked agent, who didn't put up any resistance.

As she was taken into custody, the officers found a duffle bag with $700,000 in cash stuffed into it. Apparently, helping the cartel sneak drugs across the border was a very lucrative business – but as she was about to find out during her long stretch in prison, it was a very dangerous one, too.

Of course, I was happy that we had made an arrest that had slowed down the flow of illegal drugs into the United States. But I didn't have much time to enjoy it. My career was about to take a sudden and unexpected change in direction.

Chapter Four

FROM SMUGGLING TO TRAFFICKING

O n a Friday at 3 p.m., I walked into my cubicle and found a memo telling me that as of Monday morning I was transferred to the Human Trafficking and Human Smuggling division.

I snatched the memo off my desk and marched into the office of my supervisor, Kenny Williams.

"What's going on here, Kenny?" I demanded. "What did I do to deserve this?"

He held his hands up and cocked his head. "Calm down. Calm down. I picked you to go."

I couldn't believe my ears. "But why? Don't I do everything you ask me to? Have I ever let you down?"

"No, you haven't." He gave me a half-smile, "And that's why I picked you."

I looked down at the paper in my hands. "Human trafficking? I don't even know what this is."

"Well, it's important. And it's something we're going to have to learn."

I realized that I was caught up in the growing pains caused by the merger of Customs and INS, but I didn't like it. As I said, I wasn't even sure what "human trafficking" was, and I didn't want anything to do with immigration. My desire was to get criminals off the streets and put them in prison, and what did that have to do with illegal aliens? (That's how ignorant I was in those days.)

"This will be good for your career," Kenny was saying. "Just wait and see. Of course, you'll have to learn the immigration stuff."

There wasn't anything I could do about it, so beginning on Monday morning I reported to my new job in another building. I have to admit that walking into that place didn't do much for my spirits. It was in an old INS building that had seen better days. The place wasn't exactly run-down. Let's just say it didn't have the sparkle and shine I was accustomed to. It could have used a fresh coat of paint and a bit of spit and polish.

I tried my best to act like I was happy to be there, but my Group Supervisor didn't seem to feel the same way. He didn't shake my hand or welcome me. Instead, he looked me up and down as if to say, "So who's this misfit they're sending me?"

He wasn't the only one who had a less-than welcoming attitude.

There were two agents there who had graduated from the academy six months earlier, and who seemed to rule the roost. They talked to me like I was a rookie, even though I had more experience than they did, and was about to be promoted to the rank of Senior Agent. I admit that it added to my angst when I found out that these guys had been working at Kmart before they decided to go into law enforcement, whereas I had spent several years as a Federal Probation Officer before my time at the Academy.

Nevertheless, I swallowed my pride and started working with these guys, learning everything they had to teach about smuggling and trafficking. When they saw that I had a professional attitude and that I was a hard worker, their attitude toward me improved. Together, we raided stash houses and motels full of illegal aliens that had been brought into the United States from Mexico and were waiting transport to their final destinations. We stopped trucks full of men, women and children who were being smuggled into the United States.

Before this, I hadn't realized that human smuggling was such a serious problem. Thousands of people from Mexico and other countries were being smuggled into the United States every day. Some because they wanted to be here. Many of these had paid their life savings to "coyotes" who promised to get them safely across the border. Tragically, like their friends in the drug cartels, the coyotes cared about nothing but money. At the first sign of trouble, they would often abandon their "clients," sometimes in the middle of the blazing hot desert. Hundreds of would-be immigrants have died trying to reach the United States, sometimes cooking to death or dying of thirst while locked in the trailer of an 18-wheeler.

Others were being smuggled across the border against their will. Some, who had been promised good jobs in the United States, were being sold into forced labor – often locked into the factories where they worked. Young girls – some only 13 or 14 years old – had been forced into prostitution, and told they would be killed if they tried to escape. As the parent of two young children, it broke my heart to think of young girls – and boys – suffering in this way.

After several weeks of intensive training – including many seminars, conferences, and long hours spent learning more about human trafficking, forced labor and sexual slavery – I was named head of the Human Trafficking Task Force in El Paso.

I was starting to feel more comfortable with what I was doing, and it felt gratifying to know that I was fighting against what amounted to a modern-day slave trade, freeing innocent people whose lives had been shattered by greedy criminals who had no compassion for others and no respect for human life. It was a pleasure to work with NGO's who helped rescue young girls from traffickers and worked to reunite them with their families – who provided education, counseling, safe shelter, and job training for older girls. Every time I thought about innocent children being robbed from their families, I thought of my daughter and son – and my heart broke all over again.

Unfortunately, my relationship with my supervisor had not improved. The more I saw of him in action, the more I wondered how he had been able to move up through the ranks to such an important position. He was the one fly in my ointment.

Then one day, a couple of months after my transfer into the Human Trafficking Division, I got a call from a long-time friend who wanted to know how I was doing and what was going on with the family. Then he said, "I'm going to stop by to see you day after tomorrow."

33

"Really?" I said. "That's great! But what's the occasion?"

"Well," he paused a moment. "I'm your new group supervisor."

"You're my what?" I asked.

"New group supervisor."

It was true, and I had to restrain myself from getting up and dancing around the office.

He knew who I was and what I could do. My track record spoke for itself. He respected me as a man and an agent, and that meant so much to me – especially after the way I had been treated by the man he was replacing. When he arrived, the entire atmosphere improved. He listened to my ideas, sought out my advice on difficult issues, and recognized my achievements in private and publicly. If only there had been more supervisors like him, my story would have a different outcome.

He hadn't been there too long, when he called me into a meeting in his office and told me, "We have this case, and it seems to us like you'd be the best one to handle it."

"Okay. Tell me about it."

He leaned back in his chair and put his hands behind his head. "Well, really, it's a corruption case."

I frowned, "But OIG won't be handling it?"

I knew that corruption cases were handled by the Office of Inspector General – the equivalent of a police Department's Office of Internal Affairs – and I wanted to make sure I wouldn't be stepping on anyone's toes.

He shook his head, "They've got way too much to do already."

The Special Agent in Charge went on to say that I would be working in tandem with OIG – "But you'll be the case agent. We've made it clear that you're the one in charge."

That sounded good to me.

"Then I'm in," I said. "Tell me more."

They informed me that we apparently had an agent who was working with someone in Mexico to smuggle illegal aliens into the United States. My job was to identify him, stop the smuggling operation and bring him to justice – an assignment that would take me nearly a year to complete.

For the first few weeks of my investigation, I didn't make much headway. I talked to some of the best sources I'd cultivated, but none of them seemed to know much. Then I thought of someone who seemed to know almost everything that was going on. Ernesto (not his real name) lived in the tiny town of Presidio, Texas. Presidio is a hamlet of about 5,000 people which lies on the border, about 250 miles southeast of El Paso. Despite the fact that it's one of the oldest towns in North America, tracing its history back to the 1600s, it doesn't look like much has happened there over all those years. It has a couple of motels, a few restaurants and some churches. It's a most unremarkable place. Then again, you never know where your help will come from.

I called Ernesto and told him that if he would drive over to El Paso to meet with me, I'd put him up in a hotel, pay for his meals and take care of his other expenses. He agreed, and we set up a meeting for the next day, Tuesday, at a parking lot in an industrial area on the outskirts of town. The place was secluded and quiet, far away from prying eyes. I took another agent with me, and we told Ernesto we were looking for a corrupt Border Patrol Agent who was working with someone in Mexico to smuggle illegal aliens into the United States.

He nodded as if he knew exactly what we were talking about. He told us he didn't know who the agent was, but he was pretty sure he could connect us with his partner in Mexico.

"He works out of Chihuahua City," he said. "Brags about working with an agent who lets him through the checkpoint. Pays him something like $500 a head."

Ernesto paused for a minute and pulled his cell phone out of his Jeans pocket.

"In fact, if you want me to, I can call him right now."

I hadn't expected this. "Of course," I said as I pulled my small digital tape recorder out of my jacket pocket.

He began flipping through his contacts. "Pretty sure I've got him in here somewhere. . . Oh, here he is."

35

Sure enough, the smuggler answered the phone on the second ring, and talked openly and with ease about his partnership with the agent from the Border Patrol. It all seemed too easy, so I didn't know if I could believe what I was hearing. Were we talking to the real smuggler, or someone with a huge ego who liked to talk big?

"I need to talk to him," Ernesto said, "Can you help me get in touch with him?"

"I can give him your number and let him decide if he wants to call you. But not today."

"Why not today?"

"Because he's out shooting his gun."

"Oh my God, Victor, what have we got here?"

After meeting with my supervisors and playing the recording for them, I took it to the U.S. Attorney's office in El Paso and played it for the Assistant U.S. Attorney, a woman I knew very well from my days as a Federal Probation Officer. The more she heard, the bigger her eyes got.

"We have a corrupt agent," I responded to her question.

She nodded, "What can we do to help you?"

"Well, first of all I need some help from internal affairs at the Border Patrol," I said.

"Absolutely."

She was as anxious as I was to catch this guy and get him behind bars, so she quickly agreed to give me as much help as I needed. "I'll assign an agent to work with you right away."

Within hours, I had a complete work schedule for all the Border Patrol agents in the El Paso area. As I reviewed the schedule, one thing jumped out at me. Every Tuesday, about one-third of the Border Patrol agents spent most of their day at the shooting range. It seemed obvious that the smuggler was referring to this when he said, "He's out shooting his gun." Our list of possible suspects had narrowed considerably.

The smuggler had even mentioned the guy's name when we talked to him. But, as I suspected, there was nobody by that name on the list. I wasn't surprised because I wouldn't have expected the smuggler to give us his partner's real name. But then, wait a minute. This list of agents carried their entire legal names – first, middle and last. The smuggler had referred to the agent by his middle name. We had identified our man!

Of course, we still didn't have the evidence we needed to make an arrest. As with the inspector who had been allowing drugs through the checkpoint, we needed to catch him in the act. Much work remained to be done before that could happen. Despite the sloppiness of the smuggler, the corrupt agent himself was very good at covering his tracks. It took a lot of diligent police work – including surveillance, wiretaps (which had to be approved by the federal courts, of course), installation of special cameras, and a whole lot more.

Our suspect lived in El Paso, but worked in the area of Las Cruces, New Mexico, about 45 miles north. Border Patrol agents rotate among three checkpoints in this area. Two of them are on major highways – Interstate 10, headed west toward California, and Interstate 25, going north toward Albuquerque – and Denver. Another checkpoint straddles a rural highway, which is the preferred route for local residents, who want to avoid the long lines on the freeways.

We discovered that our smuggler would come to El Paso, rent a van or a big SUV, load it up with eight or nine illegals who had been waiting at a stash house, and the crooked agent would let them drive right through the checkpoint. Most of the time they headed north on I-25 toward Denver. From there, they could go anywhere they wanted to go in the United States.

For a while, it seemed they were always one step ahead of us.

As you can imagine, we kept a close eye on our prime suspect, but he seemed to be toeing the line.

Then, our ongoing investigation revealed that the cars were being rented through a specific rental car business in El Paso. I went by the place and had a stern conversation with the manager. As nicely as I could, I informed him that I was running a police investigation and I needed his cooperation. If he did not cooperate, he could expect to be arrested on a charge of obstruction of justice.

"I'll help you in any way I can," he promised.

"We have information that the person we're seeking is going to come here sometimes within the next few days, and he'll want to rent a van or a Suburban."

"Both are available."

I thought it over for a minute and said, "I have a hunch he's going to go with the Suburban."

"Okay."

"So I want to put a tracking device on it."

"Of course."

I don't really know why I chose the Suburban. It was just that I had to pick one or the other, so in that sense it was like flipping a coin.

I called my techie and asked him to come to the lot, and installed a tracking device on the Suburban. All we could do now was wait – and we didn't have very long to do that. In fact, the Suburban was rented the very next day.

Sure enough, within a half-hour or so of leaving the rent-a-car lot, the car was on Interstate 25, heading north into New Mexico. I headed out in my own car, a Dodge Dakota that didn't look anything like an official vehicle, and quickly had the Suburban in my sights. I maintained a comfortable distance back as we headed toward the Border Patrol checkpoint. I was close enough to see that there was more than one person in that car. In fact, it looked like he had an entire mariachi band crammed into that thing.

Half a mile or so down the highway, members of the New Mexico State police were waiting to join the pursuit – although it really wasn't a pursuit. Remember that the smugglers weren't the primary the target of our investigation. We were after the Border Patrol agent who was on the take – but in order to get him, we had to find out who the agent was working for.

I was three or four cars back in the line when I saw the Suburban pass through the checkpoint. I wasn't surprised to see that our primary suspect was on duty and had waved the Suburban on past. That was one more affirmation that we were chasing the right guy. He was a young, strong guy with an athletic build – barely into his thirties. I found out later that he was a stellar soccer player, who was still playing semi-pro ball and hoping to land a spot with a professional team. But he had been taken a detour into crime.

I glanced at the clock on my dashboard and saw that it was ten minutes after twelve. I knew that the shift ended at twelve, and our suspect should have gone off duty then. But there were no signs that he was ready to leave his post. This provided us with another important piece of information. Apparently, our suspect was calling his own shots. If he wanted to work overtime. If he wanted to leave early, or trade places with another agent, he apparently did that, too. In other words, he was adjusting his own schedule to help his smuggler partners.

Suddenly, I was there at the checkpoint, his eyes looking into mine.

"Where are you headed?" he asked.

"On my way to Albuquerque," I answered.

"On business?"

I shook my head. "Going up to see my girlfriend."

"Okay. Have a nice trip." He waved for me to go on.

I was thankful that he hadn't noticed all the switches that I could use to turn my siren and flashing lights when I needed them. But I knew that several other officers were following me, and I didn't want to take any chances on tipping him off that we were closing in on him. If he knew, he could run – and we might lose him.

I got on the radio to the officers. "Stand down! Stand down!" I told them. "The guy's still at the checkpoint.

Meanwhile, the guy in the Suburban was driving the speed limit, in a brand-new car, and we didn't have any reason to stop him. Usually, you can find some reason to pull a car over — a burned-out tail-light, failing to signal when changing lanes, something. But this guy wasn't doing anything wrong. At one point, the speed limit was 75 and he was going 77. You can't pull someone over for going two miles an hour over the limit!

Finally, his foot got heavy on the accelerator and we were able to stop him for speeding. The officer who stopped him asked what he was doing with all the people in his car, and he said, "I was just giving them a ride." Not the most ingenious excuse any of us had ever heard.

We were absolutely certain now that we had the right man in our sights. But we still weren't ready to make an arrest. For one thing, we didn't know where the stash house was, and we wanted to shut it down. As I've mentioned before, a stash house is where illegal aliens are kept – sometimes going without adequate food or water, and sleeping on the floor, while they're waiting for the coyotes to take them further north. Most likely, the house we were looking for was in El Paso. After all, the hard part wasn't getting them across the border into the United States, but rather, getting them through the checkpoint and further north, where they could travel freely.

But as the net grew tighter, we were convinced that it was only a matter of time.

————

On a subsequent occasion, I called Ernesto in Presidio and told him we wanted him to pose as an illegal who needed to get to his uncle's house in Albuquerque. We told him to communicate with the smugglers and ask them to pick him up at a specific location in El Paso. Of course, we supplied him with the money he needed for the trip and gave him a tracking device. Somewhere down the road, once they had passed the checkpoint, we would pull them over. Meantime, we were listening in to the driver's cell phone conversations via a government-approved wiretap – and could hear him complaining about his passengers. He couldn't stand their stench, and was irritated that he had to make such a long drive. He was especially upset that he was going to have to spend his own money to buy them some food and drinks. "I'll get them some chips and water," he said. "That's enough for them." He obviously didn't care about them at all, or even see them as human beings. I felt he was the sort of guy who would abandon them at the first sign of trouble.

Several miles down the road, we pulled him over and then escorted the whole group to the ICE processing center in

Albuquerque, about 220 miles north of Las Cruces. They were all placed in a holding cell until they could be interviewed – and I had the "pleasure" of interrogating the driver. I had a stern, but tactful "speech" that I often used in those days, and it went something like this:

"You strike me as an honest man."

"Oh, I am sir. I really am."

"I doubt if you've ever been in trouble with the law before."

"No, sir, I haven't."

"Well, how did you wind up with all these people in your car?"

"Well, I'm just taking my friend to his uncle's house here in Albuquerque."

I had to turn away and fight to keep from laughing. The fellow was trying to feed us the story we had made up for Ernesto.

"Well, you can get in big trouble doing this, do you understand? Keep it up and you'll wind up in jail for a very long time. You don't want that to happen, do you?"

"No, sir."

"Well, I'll tell you what I'm going to do. Because I think you're an honest guy who just made a mistake, I'm going to let you go this time."

"Oh, thank you, Sir. "Thank you!"

"But I don't ever want to see you again…do you understand? If I ever see your face, there will be consequences beyond my control."

"I promise sir. You'll never see me again."

And so it went. This guy, who had sounded so tough and arrogant over the wiretap, now looked and acted like a meek little lamb. It was hilarious – and kind of sickening at the same time.

One thing the poor fellow didn't know was that while he was in there talking to me, my partner was out placing a tracking device on his car.

When I finally let him go, he ran out, jumped into his vehicle and drove straight back to the stash house in El Paso.

We were all jumping for joy, because we now knew where the stash house was – a meager nondescript stucco building in a middle-class neighborhood that was probably built in the early sixties. There wasn't anything to make a person think there was something illegal going on here – except that all the windows were covered by blinds. Obviously, whoever lived there didn't want anyone peeking inside.

The very next night – actually it was very early in the morning, about 2 a.m. — a technical crew went by the stash house and installed a camera pole so we could keep an eye on the place via our laptop computers. That is a much more convenient method of surveillance than sitting in a patrol car all night long, keeping watch through a pair of binoculars.

It wasn't very long before we got exactly what we wanted and needed.

On the following Saturday morning, I took a look at my laptop – just in time to see a late-model SUV pull up in front of the house. A closer look revealed that the car was a GMC Denali, a vehicle which retails for around $50,000.

There was something familiar about the driver of that car. He was a young man with an athletic build.

I moved closer for a better look.

At one point, he turned and looked directly at our camera. At that moment, I recognized the eyes I had looked into on the day I told him I was going to Albuquerque to visit my girlfriend. I held my breath, wondering for a moment if he knew we were watching him.

I exhaled as he turned away and headed toward the house. I had been chasing this guy for almost a year. I couldn't believe that he had actually gone to the stash house. It seemed like such a reckless thing.

"What the hell is he doing?" I was so shocked by what I saw, I said it out loud.

I watched as he went into the house, and waited several minutes for him to come back outside. I was starting to worry that he had gone out the back door and run, when he suddenly appeared again, carrying a large manilla envelope full of something that looked suspiciously like cash. As it turned out, that's exactly what it was. All the pieces of the puzzle were clearly coming together.

Over the next few days, we continued building an airtight case against him. We all agreed that when the time came to arrest him, we wanted to take him into custody while he was at work and in uniform. Everyone was in agreement about this – and by everyone, I mean my supervisor, my colleagues, the assistant U.S. attorney and me. We all figured it was an important way to send a signal to anyone else who might be tempted by the money smugglers offer. We wanted them to know that we were paying attention and would come after anyone who got on the wrong side of the law.

When the day finally came, we wanted to make sure that our suspect was disarmed before we arrested him. Otherwise, we could be putting our lives on the line. We decided to take advantage of the fact that the Border Patrol sometimes has surprise inspections. What happens is that a few of the officers are called aside and inspected to make sure their shoes are properly shined, their uniforms are just right, and their firearms are in good working order. So we chose our suspect and another agent and asked them to give us their guns so we could inspect them. And as soon as we had his gun, we arrested him.

He was belligerent at first, but when we began to handcuff him, he knew there was no use resisting, and he calmed down. All of the Border Patrol agents came out to the parking lot to watch as we loaded him into the back seat of one of our patrol cars and took him off to jail.

The arrest came on May 8, 2008. I had been investigating him since June of 2007. At the same time he was being arrested, another team was raiding the stash house in El Paso, arresting the driver and the illegals hiding there.

After his arrest, we discovered an old, corroded toilet sitting in the backyard of the house. The thing wasn't pretty. It was caked with mud, dirt and cobwebs. No way did it look like a million dollars. And yet, the smugglers were using it as a bank. Every week or so, they would stash an envelope full of money under that old appliance, and the crooked agent would come by and pick it up.

Subsequent testimony revealed that our man was getting a cool $500 for every illegal he allowed into the United States. That means one Suburban full of aliens could net as much as

$4,500. Talk about a lucrative career. But the retirement system sucks. Unless, of course, you want to spend your retirement years in prison.

By the way, several months after this incident, I was walking through our offices in El Paso when I heard someone calling me.

"Hey! Hey! I know you."

I stuck my head in one of the interrogation rooms, and there was the man I had released in Albuquerque – the one who led us to the stash house. Apparently, he had just been arrested on a smuggling charge.

He wore a big, friendly grin. "Hey, I remember you. You're the one who let me go up in Albuquerque that time. What are you doing in El Paso?"

He sounded like he thought he was talking to an old friend and that it was a strange coincidence that we should meet again this way.

I sat down and said, "Listen, the reason you're here is because of me. I've been following you for eight months!"

I have never seen a smile turn upside down so quickly.

I admit that I had a good time during much of this investigation. I enjoyed the detective work and the fulfillment that came from putting the pieces of the puzzle together. But there were other investigations that broke my heart and left me struggling to deal with man's ability to be vicious and cruel to others.

For example, I helped rescue a deaf and mute woman who had been forced into indentured servitude. She was made to clean and cook for her captors to the point where she was near exhaustion. She was repeatedly abused and even raped when her work fell short of her captors' standards. They were so abusive that they had to take her to the hospital on several occasions because she became ill. She tried to tell her doctors through sign language what was happening to her, but her captors "translated" her signing into what they wanted the doctors to hear. I was able to find her by combing hospital records, acted on a hunch, and freed her. Her testimony led to the take down of a large operation.

And then there was the physician's assistant from El Paso who often traveled to Ciudad Juarez, Mexico, to have sex with poor, underage boys. He had essentially established his own private child sex tourism service. He would drive into the city and use food, sodas, candy, money, and nice clothes to get poor boys – many of whom were living in cardboard shacks– to come into the car with him. He would then take them to a motel and rape them repeatedly. I didn't sleep for several days while I investigated this case. I combed through dozens of files, trying to find where this monster was taking the children he abducted. Finally, I was able to identify him, provide corroborating evidence, and he was subsequently sentenced to sixty years in prison in Mexico. The children were rescued and taken into child protective services.

Often, I was working on several such cases at once. Of course, I still think about the victims and pray that they are all doing well today.

During those days, even though I was satisfied to know I was helping vulnerable children and young adults, I began to feel somewhat stained by everything I witnessed during the investigations into these heinous crimes. I was constantly face to face with the worst sort of human behavior. For example, my colleagues and I had to review and analyze suspects' computers that were full of the most disturbing sort of images. It is extremely difficult to believe some of the things these monsters do to pre-pubescent boys and girls. I saw some horrific, sickening images that I can't begin to describe. Let me just say that our group of cyber-crimes agents have to go through routine counseling. That's how bad it can be when you're embedded in that nastiness, as I was.

During that time, an FBI agent was assigned to work with me as part of our task force. He worked out of my office, and I was grateful for his help and support.

Chapter Five

INTO THE FIRE

In 2008, Ciudad Juarez was named "the most dangerous city in the world," out-ranking Kabul, Afghanistan; Mogadishu, Somalia; and Baghdad, Iraq. At that time, more than 350 people were being killed in Ciudad Juarez every month due to drug-related violence. Some weekends, 50 people were killed. The cartels slaughtered countless people, left them for dead by the roadside or tossed them into mass graves, and got away with it. The police and military forces were no match for the ruthless criminals.

The city always had a place in my heart. Growing up in a border town, we often visited relatives and went out to dinner with friends in Ciudad Juarez. When I was dating Claudia, we crossed over the bridge to enjoy the legendary night life it offered. I have many fond memories of a once safe and fun city. It was almost more than I could bear to see her sinking to such depths of depravity.

But because the danger was so great there, and the situation seemed so hopeless, many of my colleagues and peers thought I had lost my mind when I applied for and was accepted into a sixty-day temporary duty (TDY) program with the ICE Office of International Affairs at the United States consulate in the city. I consciously did not inform my family of this assignment. The only persons who knew of my whereabouts were my wife and the El Paso ICE office. Life was busy enough in El Paso, but my colleagues felt that as I drove across the border and into Ciudad

Juarez each day, I was going from the proverbial frying pan and into the fire.

Sure enough, during my two-month stint in Mexico, I was overwhelmed with cases.

Things were so bad in Ciudad Juarez that within six weeks my team and I discovered several mass burial sites. The bodies of the victims were in various states of decomposition. The graves left a lasting impression on me. I will never forget all those gray, swollen corpses, dressed in ragged jeans and T-shirts. People who had apparently spent their lives in poverty, and then were slaughtered like cattle at a market. It brings me some solace to know I helped bring some of the killers to justice, but it weighs on me to know that many of the killers are still out there somewhere.

During this same period, some 300 young women – from teens to those in their early twenties — were snatched off the streets of the city and murdered. Most of the bodies were found in an isolated area called Lote Bravo. This was one of the most sickening and depressing cases I've ever been involved in, and I'm sad to say that no killer or killers were ever arrested. It remains a great, sickening mystery. According to the rumor that circulated through the city at that time, any man who wanted to get rid of a wife or girlfriend could kill her and dump her body in Lote Bravo without fear that the Mexican police would investigate. Apparently, some of the murders were related to the Occult. The girls and women were sacrificed in order to obtain demonic power.

This case was only one of many others that I had to deal with during my time in Ciudad Juarez. I scoured for and found wanted fugitives and returned them to the United States for sentencing. I worked on an arms trafficking case in coordination with the government in Mexico City. And I kept an eye on drug cartels, including Zetas who, in my mind were the most violent, corrupt and shameless of them all. All of these cases happened concurrently—a swirling whirlpool of corruption and violence that seemed as deep as the Pacific Ocean.

The citizens were not the only ones in harm's way. On March 14, 2010, after a children's birthday party that was held at the U.S. Consulate building, the cartel chased down and killed Lesley

Enriquez, a U.S. citizen and embassy employee who was four months pregnant at the time. She was driving with her husband, and their baby was in the back seat. The family tried to outrun the gunman, driving madly through the city to the U.S. border, but they didn't make it. The cartel shot and killed the adults, leaving their baby wailing in the back seat. At the same time, on the other side of town, gunmen shot and killed Jorge Alberto Salcido Ceniceros, whose wife worked at the consulate. His children, ages 2, 4 and 6, were in the car when the shooting occurred.

It wasn't until May of 2020 that the final fugitive in this case was captured by the FBI. Luis Mendez, a former member of the Barrio Azteca gang, was arrested in the city of Cuernavaca. He was identified in Mexican news reports as Luis Gerardo Mendez, alias "El Tio" (the uncle).

I was not in Ciudad Juarez when these shootings occurred, but they are examples of the continual blood-letting and horror that goes on in this once peaceful city. By this time, I had applied for and been accepted to fill a post in Mexico City. Why did I want to work there? Because I wanted to make a difference in the world, and when it came to illegal immigration and human trafficking into the United States, I figured Mexico would be the center of activity. I was right about that. But I had no idea how very busy it would be. I discovered upon my arrival that Mexico City is the busiest ICE office in the world. Yet, as busy as it was, we were woefully understaffed. In fact, I was one of only four ICE Agents in a city of more than 20 million people. By contrast, there were over 30 DEA Agents in the city.

In early November of 2008, my supervisor was scheduled to go to Mexico City to host a meeting. I asked him, "Hey, let me go with you. I've never been there." The next day he asked me if I wanted to go in his place and handle the meeting for him. I jumped at the chance.

My supervisor thought about it for a moment and then asked, "How would you feel about staying down there for a couple of weeks. They could really use some help."

It sounded like quite an adventure to me.

"Heck yeah! I'd love to."

At this time, I was temporarily working in Juarez, but still assigned to El Paso. I took several agents from El Paso along with me to Mexico City, but I stayed there after everyone else went home. I must say I had a great time in the city. An agent from Arizona, who had spent some time in Mexico's capital, told me he'd show me around – and he did. He showed me the sights of the city, from the pyramids to the main square. What a beautiful place – but with an underbelly of crime, violence and heartbreaking poverty.

When the time rolled around for me to return to El Paso, the ICE Attaché asked me to stay in Mexico City another week. I could see how busy they were, and I wanted to help them. Besides, I was so taken with the city that when a permanent position opened up, I applied. During that extra week in Mexico, I drove on Highway 57 for the first time – all the way from Mexico City to Texas. There were four armored vehicles on the trip, and the host country of Mexico had been informed of the trip. It was during that drive that the Attaché called and asked if I would come to Mexico City permanently. But before I could answer that question, he asked me another: "Is your wife on board?"

"Yes sir, she is."

He told me he was very happy to hear that. Apparently they had quite a bit of trouble with the agent's wives. What I didn't know at the time was that this came about because the men were so busy they hardly ever saw their wives and families.

One major benefit of our work situation in Mexico was that all of us were like a tight family. My colleagues seemed more like brothers than co-workers. One of the reasons for this was that there were so few of us, we really had to depend on each other in every situation. We had to have each other's backs at all time – and we did. Another reason was that we were so extremely busy. We worked long hours together, and everyone had to pull his weight. The workload put us under pressure that melded us together as a unit.

In order to move to Mexico, Claudia and the children had to make some big sacrifices. She was one of the top pharmaceutical sales representatives in the United States for her company, and I was a GS-13 senior agent. We owned a beautiful 4,000-square foot house, and Sofia and Victor were in private school, which they loved. What's more, Claudia and I both felt at home in El Paso. But at the same time, we wanted our children to have a bigger view of the world than just West Texas. We wanted them to have more of an international world view, and that, as much as anything, was our reason for taking the job in Mexico.

We had to deal with quite a bit of culture shock to make the transition to our new city, and yet, there were some things about Mexico City that we loved right from the start. One of these was our new temporary home at the Intercontinental Hotel, in the heart of the city. The five-star hotel was within walking distance of my office, which was an amazing blessing. It meant a great deal to me that I didn't have to spend hours every day trying to negotiate and survive the craziness of Mexico City's traffic. (Let me tell you, drivers in Mexico City know exactly where their horns are, but I'm not so sure about their brakes.) But the best part about being in the hotel was that Sofia and Victor were the only two children and everyday was a grand adventure! They had so much fun exploring the beautiful grounds and were spoiled by the kind staff who looked out for them and knew them by name. For them, life in Mexico was full of excitement. When we sat down and made up a list of the pros and cons regarding moving to Mexico, we came up with 252 reasons for making the move!

Speaking of the traffic in Mexico City, I recall that one of my first assignments was to go back to the airport to pick up an agent who was flying in for his TDY assignment. When our acting Attaché asked me if I could do it, I was very hesitant.

"I don't know," I admitted. "I've only been in that airport once and that was a few days ago. There were a lot of twists in turns in that trip." Not to mention that it was a really long drive – especially in heavy traffic.

My boss tore a piece of paper out of a legal pad on his desk and started scribbling.

"Follow these directions exactly, and you'll be just fine," he said.

After a couple of minutes, he handed me a map with complete directions. I'm pretty sure he had included every landmark between our office and the airport. What an amazing piece of work!

"Now I meant what I said," he told me. "Follow this <u>exactly</u>."

I did as he said, and between his map and our Garmin GPS system, I didn't have one bit of trouble. In fact, on the way back to the office, the agent that I'd picked up said, "I can see that you've been in Mexico City for a while."

"Not really," I laughed. "I've been here less than a week."

"Really?" Then how. . .?

"That's right. Take a look at this."

I showed him the map and we both marveled over our supervisor's creativity and accuracy.

———

I had been busy back home in El Paso and was often out all night as we pursued criminals. But even then, I would be able to come home during the day, get some sleep, and spend some time with Claudia and the kids. It wasn't that way in Mexico. Yes, I often worked all night — -but I worked all day, too. I had to content myself with occasional catnaps, and never got enough sleep.

I made many promises to my family that I would try to do better, but it was impossible. We literally seemed to be on the job 24/7. Even on the rare occasions when I was home at night, I would be answering phone calls and responding to emails until 1 or 2 in the morning.

For eight months, in addition to everything else, I was also taking on the duties of an assistant Attaché, because I didn't have one. Every agent was supposed to report directly to an assistant Attaché who, in turn, reported to the Attaché. That changed when Simon was appointed. We all knew that he had spent two years in Mexico earlier in his career, so we were all looking forward to his expert guidance.

Wrong!

He didn't seem to know—or even care about knowing—most of the people we had to deal with on a regular basis. When we went to meet with Mexican officials, he had no idea where to park.

In addition to that, he was an authoritarian leader with a long list of rules and an attitude. "Here's how it's going to be from now on," he told us. He must have thought he had come in to rescue a sinking ship, but the truth was that we had one heck of a team.

One afternoon, shortly after his arrival, he told me, "I go to bed at 8:30 every night, so don't bother me after that time."

I couldn't help myself. "Really? Man, you're in the wrong country because we're just getting going at 8:30 every night."

It didn't matter to him.

"I mean it," he said, "don't ever bother me after 8:30. I get up at 4:30 and I need eight hours of sleep."

The man seemed to think that taking a post in Mexico was like an early retirement. But I knew from experience that it was far from that.

As for me, I was immersing myself in the culture of Mexico. In fact, some of my Mexican counterparts I worked closely with had no idea that I was born in the United States. I had known these officials seven or eight months, but they had never heard me speak a word of English, since all our conversations were conducted in Spanish.

During a human trafficking conference in Washington, D.C., I facilitated a presentation. speech. When they heard me speaking English, their eyes almost popped out of their heads.

When I came down from the podium, one of my Mexican colleagues said, "Man, I didn't recognize you up there."

"What do you mean, you didn't recognize me?"

"Man, you were…you were speaking English?"

He said it like I had been walking on water or doing something else that was just as miraculous.

"Yes, I know," I agreed.

"I didn't know you could speak English!"

I shrugged, "I was born in the United States."

He kept shaking his head like he couldn't believe it.

Obviously, I had been away from home a bit too long.

———

One of the many things that kept us busy was our work with ICE offices all over the world. My inbox was constantly full of requests from our state offices, asking for our help in ongoing investigations. We often had agents flying into Mexico City to work with us, and we had to put aside our own investigations to help them.

As an example, one week, two agents flew in from San Diego to track down a witness investigation. A crucial witness was thought to be hiding in the jungle near Puerto Vallarta, so we took off to look for him. Now, as Americans or U.S. diplomats, we had no authority in Mexico, so we had to have a Mexican Federal Police prosecutor with us. It took several hours of driving around in the jungle before we located the witness.

On another occasion I had to take a group of four armed Federal Police Officers to the Cuernavaca area to find a witness to war crimes that had allegedly taken place in Central America — another trip that took several hours. There was also an ICE fugitive hiding out in Cuernavaca we had to find and arrest, plus I had my own trafficking investigations, administrative work, etc. There just weren't enough hours in the day.

This was a difficult time for me, because I missed so many of my children's important events. Since becoming a Special Agent, I was proud to maintain a work/life balance and carve out time for my family, but my assignment in Mexico was the exception. Sofia and Victor Emilio tried to understand and be strong. They knew Daddy's job was important, that I was trying to make the world a better place by getting bad guys off the streets, so they tried to be brave and said it was okay when I missed their award ceremonies, concerts and other occasions, Then they took as many photos and videos as they could to show me when I came home

Claudia, as always, was a rock. She was unflinchingly supportive of me – but I also saw the hurt in her eyes. I had always worked hard, but had never thought of myself as a workaholic. But I was committed to the mission and didn't know how to disconnect.

Finally, after months of working long hours every day, I had the weekend off. I don't know how that came about, but I was so excited about having 48 hours to forget about my job — to just put my feet up and take it easy.

But Claudia greeted me with a kiss as I came through the door on Friday afternoon and asked, "What are you doing this weekend?"

"Nothing," I answered.

"Fine," she smiled, "but not here."

"Not here?"

She shook her head. "No. We're going to the beach."

"The beach?" I wasn't happy about it. "Can't we just stay home?" I complained. "I'm so tired."

"If we stay home, you'll wind up spending the entire weekend on the phone – or your computer."

I started to protest, but it was no use.

"We're going to the beach. Our plane leaves in 90 minutes. And no phones."

I wasn't looking forward to another flight, for any reason. It sometimes seemed to me like I was living on an airplane in those days. I was always flying off somewhere – to Denver, Washington, Panama City, Phoenix – you name it, I've probably flown into their airport – and I had so many frequent flier miles that I could probably spend as much time circling the earth as one of our space station astronauts – but I knew better than to fight, and we compromised on my cell phones. I locked them in the hotel safe during the day, and only got them out when we came back to our room in the evening. (And yes, I admit that I was on them for a few hours every night. Certainly, Claudia was right. If I had stayed home, they would have taken up all my time.)

We had such a fantastic, memorable time, swimming, body surfing, snorkeling, and picnicking on the beach. It felt great to disconnect and enjoy my family. I could see the enthusiasm in my children's faces as they constantly yelled out, "Daddy, look at me!" while they performed some tricks in the pool or built sandcastles taller than themselves. This reminded me of how impressionable and vulnerable my kids were at the tender ages of nine and four. But all too soon, the weekend was over, and we were on our way back to Mexico City, to deal with sex traffickers and other criminals.

In fact, just before we were ready to come home, I received a call from the office, asking where I was.

"I'm on a short vacation with my family."

"Oh, man. . .Victor, we need you here!"

"We're just about to leave for the airport."

"Okay. We need to see you as soon as you get here."

"I'll be there as soon as I can."

Guilt washed over me as I knew that once we landed in Mexico City, I would resume just where I left off, and my family would once more be on the backburner.

But at the same time, duty was calling, so what could I do.

After we touched down at Mexico City International Airport, my family took a taxi home, and I took another taxi to the federal police headquarters. I didn't get home until two days later – wearing the same clothes.

————

We had a very dangerous job, and it was made even worse by the antagonism and mistrust that existed between various law enforcement agencies that were supposed to be working together. For one thing, our Attaché had done almost nothing to develop decent rapport with the Mexican authorities. And then, as I've said before, we had no real authority in Mexico, even though we worked with the Mexican police to make arrests, and often put our lives on the line. To be honest, we never knew for sure if the Mexican authorities had their own agenda during certain operations. It's an eerie feeling when you're surrounded by guns, and not totally sure if the people holding those guns are on your side.

To complicate the issue even further, there were basically two different police organizations in Mexico at the time. There were no clear lines of authority, and the two branches of law enforcement did not work particularly well together. The Mexican Attorney General's Office (PGR) did not trust the Mexican Federal Police and vice versa. In fact, PGR (traditionally in charge of criminal investigations in Mexico) never allowed the Mexican Federal Police to set foot in their building. I soon realized nothing substantial would be accomplished unless the two agencies learned how to cooperate. I spearheaded and instituted a program to bring them together and collaborate on legislation, which had never been done.

It was not easy.

I spent hours talking to both the federal police and the attorney general's office, trying to get them to unite against organized crime. In a developing country like Mexico, where so many people are struggling to get by on two or three dollars a day — and where the average cop makes about $500 a month — there is obvious potential for corruption. It didn't help that this entire time, Mexico's Secretary of Public Safety – a man we met with almost every day — was working with the Sinaloa cartel. In December of 2019, he was arrested and charged with taking millions of bribes from the cartel. Allegedly, on two occasions he received a suitcase stuffed with $3 million in cash.

Our goal was to create a vetted team of trustworthy, honest, first-rate police officers who could help liberate Mexico from the gangsters and cartels who control so much of the country. We started by asking the Mexican Federal Police to send us fifty of their best men. We would put them through a rigorous interview process, do an extensive background check and ask them to take a polygraph (lie detector) test. The polygraph was simple. It couldn't dig too deep, but rather allowed us to ask yes or no questions.

It uncovered so much corruption. Human rights violations. Use of excessive force. Unscrupulous activity.

Once our prospective officers were hooked up to that machine, their confessions came tumbling out. I recall one man who pulled the cuff off his arm, got up and ran out of the room before we even asked him a question.

Only five of the first 50 men passed our test, so we had to ask for 50 more. And 50 more after that! But we wouldn't give up. We couldn't, because the future of the Mexican people – and in many ways, the future of the United States, depended on our success.

Slowly, but steadily, our elite crime-fighting force came together.

———

It may be hard to imagine — I know it is for me — but it wasn't until 2009 that Mexico passed a law-making human trafficking a federal crime. In fact, I conducted many human trafficking conferences for police departments and prosecutors throughout Mexico. These conferences focused on techniques to investigate human trafficking, victim identification and collaboration with NGOs in an effort to combat this ever-growing horrific crime. I am proud to be responsible for dismantling several sex trafficking rings which operated out of Mexico.

Some tactics used by these scumbags included recruitment of young girls – barely into their teens – by promising them good-paying jobs in New York City, offering to reunite them with family in the United States, and sometimes even offering to marry them and make them American citizens. Instead, they were placed into squalid, disgusting brothels where they were "entertaining" anywhere between 20 and 30 Johns a day. Each "customer" paid $75, which means the girls were bringing in thousands of dollars, but they never saw a penny of it. They were barely given enough to eat, received no medical care, and continued to work until they became too weak, exhausted or sick to continue.

After that, they were tossed out to fend for themselves, and some died on the streets.

Meanwhile, if the girls did anything that displeased their traffickers – like trying to escape, they were severely beaten, burned with cigarettes, or worse. One of these girls had a baby, and her captors placed the new-born in a bucket, filled it with cement and left it in her room as a warning to her and the other girls. This shows the viciousness used to break down the girls physically and emotionally. Those human-trafficking victims were too terrified and afraid to try to escape. I'm not an emotional guy, but it brings tears to my eyes to think of what those young girls endured. They were broken in spirit, completely separated from the people they loved, and endured constant abuse.

My only relief comes from knowing that their tormentors were sentenced to long prison sentences. I hope they never get out.

On another occasion, in Miami, we rescued two young Mexican girls from a similar situation.

I told the Mexican Federal Police, who were going to interview the girls at the Mexican consulate in Miami, about what they had been through. One of these was a hard-nosed, tough-as-nails mean-looking guy who had been a cop for 30 years. This guy was battle-scarred, and he looked like nothing could phase him. I told him, "Listen, you have to be very careful how you talk to these girls, because they are deeply traumatized."

He shot me a look like, "Who are you to be telling me what to do?"

He and his partner spent several hours interviewing the victims and documenting what they had been through. When he came out of the interview room, his tough look was gone. He looked at me with tears of anger in his eyes. "Victor," he said, "I'm going to do everything I can to help you get these sons of bitches."

And he did. They, too, are in prison right now."

———

Shortly after this, we began working on a criminal investigation called Operation in Plain Sight. The operation was a top-priority case involving a large-scale criminal organization that smuggled humans, weapons, and narcotics, while also running a seamless money laundering service. The organization operated on both sides of the border – in Sonora, Mexico, and southern Arizona – especially in the Nogales area. This particular organization was best known for smuggling illegal aliens across the border in vehicles that were painted to look like medical transport vans. Along the Arizona border, there are many patients who travel to hospitals in Mexico for treatment, so it didn't arouse any suspicion to see one of these vehicles coming across the border.

We had identified many of the main players but needed the full cooperation from agencies in both the U.S. and Mexico to take them down. This was the first time that ICE worked with both the Mexican Police and the Mexican Attorney General's Office

(PGR). Our goal was to conduct raids in Arizona and Mexico simultaneously, and get these criminals off the streets.

As case agent for this takedown, I was sent to Arizona to brief ICE agents in Phoenix and Tucson. For the operation to be successful, everyone had to work together seamlessly. We all needed to know our roles and perform them in perfect synchronization. While, in Phoenix, I got a pleasant surprise when one of my oldest and closest friends walked into the conference room. I had known him since my time at the Academy. He was the one who had brought such joy and relief to me when he was selected as my group supervisor, shortly after I began working for the Human Trafficking Division. I had lost touch with him and had no idea that he was now Director of Operations for ICE and had flown in from Washington for our meeting.

"Victor," he told me, "I'm hearing your name everywhere I go!"

"Well, I hope they're saying good things," I joked.

"The best," he smiled. "They tell me you're it in Mexico. This case depends on you."

I wasn't sure how to respond, so I just thanked him for his support.

"I'm just glad to know that everything is in your capable hands."

I was determined to live up to the confidence he had placed in me.

As it turned out, Operation in Plain Sight was an extremely successful operation. But it sure didn't start that way.

———

It took a couple more months to put the pieces together, but finally, we were ready to roll. The plan was to fly from Mexico City to Hermosillo. From there, we would cover the last 180 miles or so to Nogales by helicopter. Just before the big day came, our office welcomed a new deputy Attaché. The Deputy Attaché was big – about 6-5 – and athletic. We called him Blue-52 because he looked so much like Hall of Fame NFL quarterback Peyton Manning. (Blue-52 was one of the plays Manning frequently called when he was behind center for the Indianapolis Colts and later the Denver Broncos.) Our Blue-52 was fairly young, too, so we figured he must be smart to have advanced so far in such a short time. He spoke only a few words of Spanish when he first joined us in Mexico, so ICE sent him to live with a family in Cuernavaca for six months to learn the language. I was surprised to find out about this special treatment, but figured he must have a lot of other skills. I wasn't happy when I was told to take Blue-52 along on this important mission – since he was new and hadn't been in on any of the planning – but I was told to follow orders, and not for the last time.

Still, I was excited when time came for us to go. We all boarded the helicopter in Mexico City, and prepared for our flight to Hermosillo. We all had our gear, our guns, our vests, our boots, and our faces were covered. The rotors were whirring, the door was up – and then I noticed something. There were no representatives of the PGR on board.

"Hey," I shouted, "wait a minute! Where's the prosecutor's office?"

"The who?"

"The prosecutor's office," I answered. "We can't go without them. Where are they?"

"Oh, well, I don't know," somebody said. "We didn't tell them about this."

My mouth dropped open. "What do you mean we didn't tell them? We don't have any authority to do this without their approval. I'm not going to have this fall apart on a technicality."

Suddenly, Blue-52 spoke up.

"What the hell is going on?"

"We can't go arrest people without the prosecutor's approval," I explained. "We have to have them with us. There are very strict laws in Mexico."

The rotors whined as they slowed to a stop, the doors opened, and we got off the aircraft.

As soon as I could find a private place, I made a call to the PGR and told them what we were doing.

They responded that they would send someone right over – a person that was known as a Magisterial Prosecutor — and he or she would be joining us in our flight to Hermosillo.

What they didn't tell us was that they were also sending a whole regiment of other people. There were photographers, the evidence team, forensics people. When the group arrived, I was astounded. Now there were way too many of us to fit into the helicopter.

After three or four hours of trying to figure out what to do, it was decided that we would fly to Hermosillo in a 747 jet which was owned by the federal police.

From there we used armored vehicles to drive to Nogales, Mexico, which is just across the border from Nogales, Arizona.

It was nearly one in the morning by the time we reached our destination, a once- flashy hotel that had fallen into disrepair. You can imagination my humiliation when Blue-52 and I were given the last available room – the honeymoon suite. As we trudged up to the room, he said to me, "You can have the master bedroom. I'll sleep on the pullout couch." Hmmmm. Maybe he wasn't such a bad guy after all.

Unfortunately, our strange adventure hadn't yet come to an end.

I slept fitfully that night, as you can imagine. So, I was shocked when I took a look at my Blackberry and saw that it was 6 a.m.

Oh, no! How in the world had that happened? I had overslept."

I ran into the other room, and saw that Blue-52 was still asleep.

"Get up!" I shouted. "Get up! We overslept!"

"Huh...Wha...."

"It's six o'clock! We're late."

He sat up in bed.

"Run down and tell everyone we'll be there as soon as possible! I'm going to jump in the shower for two minutes."

Blue-52 jumped up and began pulling on his pants and shirt. Two minutes later, as I was just getting out of the shower, I heard him coming back into the room."

"What's up?" I called out.

"It's four o'clock," he shouted as he crawled back into bed."

"What?" That's when it hit me. I had expected my Blackberry to automatically reset to reflect the time difference between Mexico City and Nogales, but it didn't.

What else could go wrong?

When the real 6 o'clock rolled around, we discovered that we didn't have any arrest warrants. The judge had signed them, but had not sent them to us and, it was said, we had to have the originals. They would have to be flown up to us, which meant another delay of several hours.

"Why do we have to have the originals," I asked one of the prosecutors.

He shrugged, "It's just the way we've always done it."

"Well, can't we just ask them to fax it to us?"

After a long discussion, we decided to have everything faxed. We approached the concierge and asked if the hotel had a fax machine.

"Certainly," he smiled.

"Well, can you give us the number."

"Well, you see, there's a bit of a problem."

"Problem?"

"We don't have any paper right now."

I don't know how we found the paper, but we managed somehow. The necessary documents were soon in our possession and I gave the signal. In several different locations across two countries, officers burst into flagged buildings all on the same day at the same time. This precision and coordination meant that no one in the smuggling ring could be alerted and flee. Over 300 criminals were arrested in Arizona that day, as well as the four leaders of the smuggling ring in Mexico.

I'm proud to say that I received the Director's Award for that operation. I think it means more to me than any other award, because I got it prior to the shooting. I got several awards after getting shot, but this one meant that I was appreciated for my service — for my work as an agent. And to me, that's the highest, most-coveted award a person can get.

Chapter Six

AGENT UNDER FIRE: MURDER ON HIGHWAY 57

C laudia held all three of my cell phones over the open toilet. Two of them were ringing. "You're done," she said. It was nearly 7 p.m. on Sunday evening and my phones had been ringing non-stop.

My wife had threatened to flush my phones down the toilet before, but she usually doled out the threat with a smirk. This time, I couldn't find even the hint of a smile. This time, she might actually drop them in.

"Those phones are expensive." I took a step toward her.

"You've been home a total of four days this year. Four days—that's it, Victor. I understand you can't always control your schedule, but this is too much."

The third phone buzzed, indicating I'd received a text message. Claudia's eyes flashed. "Even when you're at home, you're at work."

"I'll turn them off." I held out open palms in supplication and surrender.

It was a few days before New Year's Day, 2011, and I had promised Claudia that I was going to cut way back on the business travel. In fact, that was my one and only New Year's resolution. But sadly, it wasn't working out as I had hoped. Over the past few weeks I had been traveling almost constantly. And I wasn't always "there" when I was at home. In just the last month and a half, I had been on five international trips for a Special Interest Alien (SIA) investigation that focused on a ring smuggling potential terrorists into the U.S. from Mexico. Some of the airport security staff at the Mexico City International Airport saw me so often they knew me by name. To make matters worse, I was scheduled to leave at five o'clock the next morning to go abroad ... again.

Claudia considered the phones and then my outstretched hands. "I have a better idea." In one fluid movement, she put the phones on the counter, pushed me out of the bathroom, and locked the door behind us. "You're not going to answer any calls for the rest of the evening."

A chorus of muffled buzzing and ringing filtered through the closed door. Someone was really trying to get in touch with me, but I forced myself to hold still.

Claudia still stood, hands locked on her hips in a determined stance, in front of the bathroom door. Her fiery, indignant attitude might have made me laugh if it hadn't been so justified. She was right. I had been neglecting her and the kids.

"All right," I agreed. "No phones tonight."

———

Six weeks later — I trudged up the stairs to our apartment, my suitcase dragging behind me. It was 1:00 am on Monday, February 14, 2011 — Valentine's Day. I had just come in from Arizona.

The trip had taken a lot out of me. I was dog tired — not because the work had been grueling, but because I had been worrying about Claudia the entire time. My long absences weren't making things between us any better.

I put my key in the lock and wiggled the door open. The house was dark inside. Everyone slept. Struck by the sensation that I was sneaking into my own home, I felt like a trespasser, a creature of the night operating under cover of darkness. Guilt wrapped itself around my shoulders, weighing me down even more.

Secretly, I loved every minute of my busy work life — the covert operations, the private jets, the high-end hotels, the dinners at five-star restaurants with foreign dignitaries. I loved that people came to me with the most difficult criminal investigations and asked for my feedback. I was proud that I represented the agency in front of congressional committees. I loved that my work received international attention and acclaim.

I pulled my suitcase inside the apartment and tiptoed my way to the master bedroom. Even in sleep, Claudia looked frazzled — as if she were running errands in her dreams.

She must have felt the demotion in my life. She hadn't been my top priority for some time. I would make it up to her — today — Valentine's Day.

My workday began at 8:00 am. I tackled the mountain of paperwork that had accumulated in my absence. I planned to knock out a few reports and leave at a reasonable hour so I could treat Claudia to a romantic dinner at our favorite sushi restaurant. A table for two by the window overlooking the rock gardens would get me bonus points. Visions of Claudia in a red dress (looking oh-so-sexy beneath the dim lights) filled my head.

Unfortunately, my supervisor had other plans.

It was nearly 2 p.m., which was usually lunch time in Mexico, and I was elbow-deep in paperwork when a co-worker, Marco, approached me. I had met Marco at the Academy and considered him to be a good friend.

"I'm headed to lunch. Want to join?" he asked.

I wasn't sure I had time for lunch. I picked up my small, spiral notebook and looked over my to-do list. It was three pages long.

"Come on, man," he urged me. "You've gotta eat."

He was right. And I was hungry, so I went along. But when we got to the restaurant, he told me something that ruined my appetite.

"Hey, dude. I just wanted to give you a heads up," he said. "The boss is planning to send you to Monterrey."

"What the hell? Why is he sending me?" I almost yelled. "I just got back!"

"I don't know, man," he shrugged, clapping his hand on my shoulder in sympathy. "I just heard about it in passing and thought you should know."

"That's fricking ridiculous. I've been out of the office non-stop. Why can't someone else go?" I could hear myself throwing a tantrum, but I'd known Marco since the academy, and we'd become close friends. He would forgive my tirade.

It was around 3:00 by the time we got back to office and I decided to confront Simon, my supervisor, right away. I found him in his office, tapping away on the keyboard. He called me in to give me assignment.

Simon was small, thin, and mild-mannered as a mouse—a man who didn't swear at all, making him an outcast in an office full of potty mouths. He avoided conflict and, as a result, wasn't effective at resolving problems or managing his team.

Unfortunately, the chain of command was strict in the HSI office. If I wanted to challenge an assignment, Simon was the one I had to talk to. Then he would present my request to Blue-52, who was his immediate supervisor.

I knocked on Simon's open door and cleared my throat.

"Hey, Victor. I actually need to talk to you." He pushed his chair back from the computer and turned to face me.

"I heard." I folded my arms. "Look, I can't go on another trip right now. I've been away too much lately."

Simon shrugged apologetically. "I'm sorry, but you don't have a choice. Blue 52 wants the equipment right away."

"Equipment?"

"Yeah, we need you to pick up some equipment for Operation Pacific Rim."

Pacific Rim was the largest money-laundering case ICE had ever seen—but I hadn't touched it. I had more than enough work with the twenty or so cases I was handling on my own. The idea that they'd send me on a mission for a case that wasn't mine irked me in more ways than I could count.

"It's not my call," he said, shrinking into his chair. "You leave tomorrow with Jaime Zapata. He's here on TDY."

"Wait." I couldn't believe what I was hearing. "You're sending us without an escort? And there's a ban on traveling Highway 57."

"Yeah, I hear you." He fiddled with the papers on his desk, absent-mindedly stacking and unstacking them into different piles. "Blue 52 still wants it done."

I threw my hands up in disbelief and suggested another option. "Why don't we get the equipment delivered via dip pouch? It's safer."

"Well, we talked about that, but he wants the equipment as soon as possible." He accidentally dropped the papers. They scattered across his desk and settled. Instead of picking them up again, he looked at his watch, as if realizing for the first time that it was past noon. "He wanted it today, but I guess tomorrow will have to do, seeing as Monterrey is eleven hours away."

I took a few more steps into the room and stood over him. "Simon, you know this isn't a good idea. There have been attacks on that highway recently."

"Look, Victor, I don't know what to tell you." He tipped his head in the direction of Jack's office, which was diagonally across the hall.

I followed Simon's gaze. Through the office window I could see Jack, Blue-52, and the two agents who were working on the Pacific Rim case in serious discussion behind closed doors.

"If you want me to approach them with your concerns, I will," said Simon. "But I'm pretty sure their minds are made up."

I weighed my options. To get what I wanted, I needed more evidence that the trip was too dangerous to undertake.

"Let's call David at the Monterrey office and ask him what he thinks about the plan," I suggested. David was a straight shooter. He'd give us an honest answer, the smart answer.

David picked up the phone right away, answering in Spanish with a Texas drawl. "What's up, *vato*?" he said, using the Mexican slang for 'man.'

"Hey, David. My office wants to send me out to Monterrey to pick up that equipment."

"You guys are crazy, man! No one should be on Highway 57 right now. It's a shit show.' He described the recent attacks, strongly advising against the journey. "Why can't we send it by dip pouch or by plane?"

"That's what I said. I don't understand why they're making us do it this way," I said.

Using David's analysis as fuel, I encouraged Simon to approach Blue-52 on my behalf.

We walked the three steps to Jack's office, and Simon tapped on the door, interrupting the meeting with Blue-52 and the Pacific Rim agents. Blue-52 quickly stepped into the hall and closed the door behind him with a whoosh. He seemed to be in a pissy mood. Just my luck.

"What's going on?" he asked abruptly.

Simon eyed the closed door. "We just got off the phone with David. He says it's not safe to drive on the road. Can we get the equipment another way?" The words ran together and away like a confused mouse skittering across a kitchen floor.

"Don't you think we talked about other ways?" Blue 52 bellowed.

"Yes, but did you know about the security issues? There's a lot of friction between the police and the Zetas Cartel in that area right now."

Blue 52 stretched to his full height, towering over Simon. "I don't know what security issues you're talking about. This is the first I've heard of them. All I know is that I want that equipment by the close of business day tomorrow." And, with that, he went back into the office and shut the door.

Simon turned to me and shrugged, "Well, there's your answer. I tried." Then he scurried back to his desk.

Later that afternoon, I met my partner for the following day's adventure. Agent Jaime Zapata was a young man with dark, cropped hair, a relaxed posture, and a friendly disposition that made you feel like he was an old friend. I was glad about that, because at least the drive together should be a pleasant one. I had lucked out in terms of getting a decent traveling companion. I liked him immediately.

After meeting Jaime, I called David to tell him the news. While he wasn't any happier about the situation than I was, we had to follow orders or risk losing our jobs to insubordination. We negotiated for a while and agreed that his team and my team would start driving around six o'clock the next morning and meet somewhere in the middle to exchange the equipment. That way, we would be back in Mexico City with the equipment before the close of the business day. That settled, I had to break the news to Claudia.

I made a mental note to soften my voice over the phone so Claudia wouldn't detect my anger and frustration. Taking a deep breath, I picked up the phone and dialed home.

"Hi, babe," I said.

"What's wrong?" she asked.

Shit. I couldn't get anything past her.

"Work stuff," I sighed. "Listen, I'm going to get home later than expected. And now I have to leave early tomorrow morning for a quick trip."

"You're leaving? But you just got back!"

"I know, I know." Anger flared in my voice, and I tried to rein it in. "It's only a day trip. I'll be back in the evening. But about tonight ... going out probably isn't the best idea. I'm not sure what time I'll be able to get out of here."

"That's okay."

I knew she was lying, trying to spare my feelings. Her voice sounded vacant, like the last echo in an empty room, a senseless repetition.

"I'm so sorry, Claudia." I knew full well an apology wouldn't be enough to make up for the time away.

Neither of us spoke for a moment.

Claudia cleared her throat, as if choking down the news and burying it. "Why don't we just have a nice quiet evening with the kids?" She sounded too cheerful.

"That sounds nice. I'll see you when I get home." I hung up, and a feeling of defeat washed over me. I picked up my to-do list again, flicked through the pages, and sighed. How many more times would I have to disappoint my wife this year?

I managed to leave the office around 7:00 and picked up some calla lilies on the way home – Claudia's favorite flower. Their beauty reminded me of hope, the kind of hope that starts as a small promise and then blooms.

When I arrived at the apartment, the kids greeted me at the door. They both wore black pants and white dress shirts. Sofia had a white tea towel folded carefully over her arm.

"Come in, Mr. Avila. Reservation for two?" she asked. She took my arm and led me to the living room, where Claudia waited. A black cocktail dress hugged her body, then flared at the waist. She looked so beautiful standing there—bold like a black brush stroke against a white canvas.

Victor Emilio, who had followed me into the room, cleared his throat. "Your table will be ready in just a moment, Mr. and Mrs. Avila."

"Why, thank you, sir." I picked up the game and played along. The kids giggled and hustled out of the room.

"You couldn't go to the restaurant," Claudia said, "so we brought the restaurant to you."

I handed her the flowers, which now looked slightly limp. "I don't deserve all this."

She shuttled the flowers to a vase atop the mantel and arranged them to her satisfaction before sitting on the couch. I joined her.

We sat quietly, gazing at each other, while the kids and the nanny bustled in the background.

"We've missed you," she said.

"I know."

"What happened at work today?" Claudia kept her eyes on mine.

"Let's talk about it later. I don't want to spoil the moment." I reached for her hand, and she let me take it.

"Ahem." Victor Emilio stood in the doorway. He made a grand, sweeping gesture with his arm and stepped to the side. "Your table awaits."

Hand in hand, Claudia and I walked into the dining room. The table, set with iridescent placemats, wine glasses, and gold-rimmed china, glowed beneath the candlelight. In the middle a carefully handwritten menu lay in the center of each plate listing appetizers, main dishes, and desserts—all from our favorite sushi restaurant. A vase filled with red roses, much fuller and more splendid than the bouquet I'd brought Claudia, served as the centerpiece. As we took it all in, our young waiter and waitress grinned ear-to-ear and perched expectantly on their toes.

"I can't believe you guys pulled this all together in one afternoon!" I said, hoping my admiration and gratitude showed in my voice.

"May I pour you some wine?" asked Sofia in a professional manner.

"Yes, please." My wife and I sat down, and Sofia filled our glasses.

"I have something for you," said Claudia, a hint of excitement in her voice. Reaching behind the flowers, she handed me a small gift-wrapped box.

My hands shook as I tore off the gold paper and opened the box. A titanium bracelet from Tiffany's lay inside—the perfect gift. I knew Claudia meant the bracelet as a symbol. It was her sweet way of saying she was still with me and that her love was still strong and unending.

I strapped the bracelet around my wrist and gazed at her sadly.

"What's the matter? Don't you like it?"

"No, no, I love it," I said. "It's perfect. It's just … I don't have anything for you." I had been in the habit of buying Claudia and the children expensive gifts to compensate for being away so often—designer purses, dresses, shoes, jewelry, toys—but I had forgotten a gift for Valentine's Day. Of all days!

"You spoil us, Victor," Claudia said. "We only need you tonight."

I went to her, closing the space between us, and kissed her fully on the mouth.

The children served us throughout the evening. We laughed. We talked. We ate. We sipped wine. We loved. The magical moments imprinted on my memory—and I would return to them over and over again when I needed comfort.

Claudia couldn't hide her distress when I told her about my assignment later that evening. We lay in bed, and I cradled her in the crook of my arm, her head against my chest.

"Why aren't the agents on the case picking up the equipment?" she asked. "Why are they sending you?"

"I don't know." I sighed in frustration. "I'm going to drive out with a new agent, Jaime Zapata. They want the equipment before the close of business tomorrow."

She lifted her head and looked at me. "Who else is going?"

"No one."

"It's just you two? No other agents? Isn't it dangerous to go without an escort?"

"I asked my supervisor those same questions, but they're still insisting I go. If I don't, they could write me up for insubordination."

"It just doesn't seem right," she said, her unease evident.

"I know." I tightened my hold on her, pulling her closer.

I checked in on the kids before leaving the next morning. Victor Emilio was still asleep, his breathing steady and deep. My heart in my throat, I kissed him gently, then went to Sofia. She was wide awake.

"Why are you going out of town again?"

"No, no," I assured her. "I'm just going to work. I'll be back tonight."

She eyed me suspiciously. "You're not wearing a suit. You always wear a suit when you're going to the embassy. You're going out of town."

Her perceptiveness startled me. Though she was right, I lied.

"No, I'm just going to work. I'll see you tonight," I said and kissed her goodbye.

I prayed I was right.

***

On the morning of our trip, another TDYer from the Laredo office brought Jaime by my apartment. He shook my hand, looked me in the eye, and grinned. "Well, let's get this over with."

I kissed Claudia goodbye, and Jaime and I hopped into the SUV provided by the agency. I took my place behind the wheel, and Jaime settled into the passenger seat. Weighing over five tons because of all the upgrades—bulletproof glass, armored body, two-way radios, etc.—they were difficult to maneuver. They took a long time to accelerate and a long time to come to a full stop.

Under most circumstances, the fact that Jaime and I didn't know much about each other would have made for a long and potentially awkward twelve-hour drive. Fortunately, Jaime was talkative and open. He was 32 years old and his fiancée, Stacye, was in dental school. Jaime's three brothers were all in law enforcement, and his father was a retired sheriff. It was obvious they were a close-knit family. We talked as if we had known each other for years.

"The hours are really a killer," I said. "I thought I worked a lot in El Paso, but my hours here have nearly doubled."

"I hear ya, *güey*," he said, "I'm considering a longer-term assignment in Mexico, but I'm not sure how my fiancée, Stacye, would handle it. She says she'd be fine, but in the end, I'm sure she'd get lonely."

"Well, the one good thing about Mexico is that the wives all get together to support each other. It's a really close-knit family. She wouldn't see you all that much, but she wouldn't be alone either."

"Yes … that makes sense." Jaime drummed his fingers on the dashboard. "How does Claudia handle it?"

I winced. "She's supportive, but it's hard on her."

"I hear ya."

I eyed him. "You sound like you're from around here. What's your story?"

"I was born in Brownsville, Texas, but my parents are from Mexico. You?"

"Same. Born in El Paso. Parents from Chihuahua." I shifted my weight and looked out at the long road ahead. The sun was still rising, hitting the pavement at a shallow angle. Bright rays reflected causing me to squint. I pushed up my sunglasses.

"Did you ever struggle with figuring out how to be loyal to both cultures … I mean, being in a border town it seemed I was being pulled in two directions—like I had to choose one or the other. You know?" Why was I telling Jaime about my childhood and adolescent struggles with identity? I didn't talk about such things often, but something about his laid-back demeanor and his accent reminded me of the boys from my hometown, and the question just came out.

He rubbed his chin thoughtfully. "Yeah. Growing up in a border town was always push and pull. Even in elementary school, the boys formed gangs or clubs that identified with a specific nationality, cultural feature, or physical trait."

"I remember those wannabe gangs. They sure were something." I chuckled.

"Yeah." Jaime grinned, but his grin faded. "Unfortunately, a lot of those kids became gang members. In the end, I decided it was better to be loyal to myself and my ideals than to something external."

"That's exactly how I reconciled it. But getting to that point was difficult."

Jaime turned to me. "But you made it."

"Yes, I made it."

Soon after, we passed a rest area with a Subway. Jaime sat up straighter, his eyes locked on the building. "They have Subway here?"

"Yeah, of course. They have a lot of American fast-food restaurants here."

"Can we stop there for lunch?" he said with a hint of excitement.

I looked at Jaime sideways and lifted my eyebrows. "You have a thing for Subway, huh?"

"Well, she's not as pretty as Stacye, but she satisfies an empty stomach."

I laughed and shook my head. "Sure thing. We'll stop on the way back."

About halfway to the meeting point, we stopped at a convenience store to gas up and get some snacks. As I pulled up to the rusty gas tanks, I scoped the scene. A heavy-set woman stood at a nearby tank, filling her brown Honda Accord, which had a dented bumper and a smashed tail light. Inside the store, a man wearing a trucker's cap was buying a pack of Marlboro's, while the attendant, a teenage boy sporting a *Cafe Tacuba* t-shirt, worked the cash register with a bored expression on his face. Nothing seemed out of the ordinary, so I unlocked the doors.

"Why don't you get us some snacks? I'll fill her up." I kept my eyes on Jaime while he went into the store. The trucker nodded to him on his way out. He seemed friendly. Still, I watched the man until he turned the corner and disappeared behind the building.

When Jaime climbed back into the SUV, I locked the doors and pulled out the backpack I had hidden behind my seat. I unzipped it and held it out to Jaime. "Take a look," I said. Inside were two fully loaded guns (a Glock 19 and a Sig Sauer 229), a radio, and a clean cell phone.

Jaime stared at me. Technically, as U.S. special agents, we were not supposed to carry weapons in Mexico. But because of our diplomatic status, we were granted special permission by the U.S. Ambassador at the U.S. Embassy. During the reign of the drug cartels, it simply wasn't smart to be without a weapon. Since we had diplomatic immunity, we were never searched, so our weapons stayed safely hidden at all times. However, Jaime did not have guns issued to him because he was only on TDY and had not been granted diplomatic status.

"Just in case the shit hits the fan," I said, pointing to the guns.

He nodded. "All right."

I tucked the backpack behind my seat and pulled back onto the highway.

We made contact with the Monterrey agents at kilometer 100. Nearby, there was a nice restaurant—a clean one with restrooms—a safe place to meet. As I turned into the parking lot, I noticed an agency suburban toward the back of the lot and pulled up next to it. Two agents promptly got out and opened the trunk. Boxes and equipment filled it to the brim.

"Shit! Is all of this stuff going to fit?" I asked.

"There's only one way to find out," said Jaime.

We got straight to work. I lowered the back seats to extend our trunk space while Jaime grabbed the first couple boxes. In the end, we managed to fit it all in, but we had to press the boxes up against the backs of our seats so we could close the trunk.

With the task completed, I asked Jaime if he wanted to eat lunch at the diner before hitting the road again.

"No thanks. I'll just wait for Subway," he said.

My stomach grumbled. "All right, but we won't be there for a couple of hours."

"I'm fine with that."

I shook my head. "I guess I really can't get between a man and his sandwich."

We hit the road again. Almost immediately, Jaime received a call on his government-issue cell phone from the Laredo office. Border agents had stopped a vehicle with a load of drugs. They wanted Jamie to arrest and process the smugglers.

"I can't respond right now. I'm on TDY in Mexico. Contact another agent to work the load for me," Jaime said.

Jaime apparently didn't shy away from extra work. I was impressed. The way he talked to the agent on the other end of the line reminded me of a younger version of myself. He was a pro-active agent, not a reactive one—the kind of agent who spotted and solved problems before others did.

"Good work, man," I said to Jaime when he hung up the phone.

He threw a lopsided grin back at me, and we lapsed into a comfortable silence.

An hour or so later, traffic slowed. I looked ahead. A federal policeman stood in the middle of the highway. Tall and broad, he had a long gun strapped across his shoulder and raised to ready position. The *federale* moved the muzzle slowly right to left, left to right, right to left, as cars slowly eked past him. He didn't stop any vehicles but looked into each intently, as if searching for something ... or someone.

I gripped the steering wheel and followed the mass of cars.

Maybe it was my imagination, but I swore a shadow darkened the man's eyes as we passed, and a smirk tugged at the corners of his lips—but he didn't flag us down.

Once we were safely past the end of his long gun, I looked over at Jaime. "That was weird."

He nodded, his fists clenched in his lap.

"Scared?" I asked.

"Yeah, man. What was that guy doing there?"

"I don't know. I've gone through all sorts of checkpoints, and I've never seen a *federale* do anything like that before." The muscles in my shoulders and neck tensed, crimping and curling like a cat before a pounce.

We got to the rest area around 1:30 p.m. and found it unusually empty. Because the bathrooms were clean and well-kept, the station typically bustled with the comings and goings of many travelers. But this afternoon, only one other car—an SUV with Texas plates—was parked on the highway side near Subway.

The emptiness gave me pause. I looked around. Someone inside mopped the floors outside the restrooms, and a couple of young people worked behind the sandwich counter. An attractive red-haired woman with gold-rimmed sunglasses occupied the SUV, chatting animatedly on her cell phone.

Jaime hopped out of the vehicle, and I followed him inside.

After washing up, we ordered our sandwiches and then took them outside to one of the small tables in front of the restaurant. Smog typically hid the Sierra Madre Oriental, but today the winds had chased the sooty clouds away and we were blessed with a remarkably clear blue sky. We could see the mountain range and Popocatépetl etched against the horizon. The quiet, which had been stifling at first, settled comfortably around us as we ate.

Jaime finished his sandwich, then wadded up the wrapper and pushed back his chair.

I threw him the keys. "Why don't you take it for a spin?" Because armored SUVs weighed 11,000 pounds, the open road was the safest place to practice driving. "We'll be on the highway for a couple more hours, and we can switch again once we hit the city and rush hour. This will be good practice for you."

He swirled the key ring around his finger. "Sweet! I'm ready."

We went out to the SUV. Jaime climbed into the driver's seat, and I gave him a quick tutorial before we got back onto the highway.

For the next 10 or 15 minutes, while Jaime drove, I was busy on my phone, sending emails, checking messages.

Suddenly, in the side mirror, Jaime noticed two SUVs coming up fast behind us. Each one appeared to be packed with people, although we couldn't make out anyone clearly.

"We've got company."

I looked in the rearview mirror, but the view was blocked due to all the boxes stacked up the back of our vehicle.

The two Suburbans flashed past us almost as if we were standing still.

In the second one, Jaime saw the silhouette of a long gun, sticking up between the seats.

"Let them go!" I said. "Just let them go."

Quickly, they were out of site and we both sighed with relief.

Then, all of a sudden, we had caught up to them. They had slowed down from about 90 to 25 miles per hour and were obviously waiting for us.

"What should I do?" Jaime asked.

"Don't stop! Keep going."

We started to pass them, but one of the SUVs sped up and matched our pace. The shooters rolled down the windows and the gunmen emerged, pointing their AK-47s directly at us.

"Pull over!" one of them yelled in Spanish. "Pull over!"

"No, don't pull over! Keep going! Keep going!" I shouted.

Jaime accelerated, trying to break free of the gunmen, but our vehicle was so heavy and slow to maneuver that they caught up easily and kept pace with us. When Jaime sped up, they sped up. When Jaime slowed down, they slowed down. All the while, one of the SUVs was next to us, with guns pointed out the passenger windows in our direction.

"Pull over!" the man demanded again.

We didn't comply.

He waved, and the first SUV pulled in front of us while the second vehicle drove beside us. Together, they slowed down, forcing us to a stop. I knew the move—a rolling roadblock—a maneuver we had been taught at the ICE Academy.

Jaimie slammed on the brakes, and we skidded to a hard stop. Even though I was wearing a seatbelt, my body smashed hard into the console. Although I didn't realize it at the time, I had dislocated my shoulder, creating a problem that would result in years of pain and require corrective surgery.

As soon as we came to a stop, the gunmen flew out of the vehicles and swiftly formed a u-shape in front of us. They positioned their guns, aiming them directly at our faces.

We raised our hands, although I have no idea how I did it with that badly injured shoulder.

"I'm going to tell you one more time—get out of the car!"

"Don't get out of the car, Jaime! Don't do it!"

"Get out of the car, motherfuckers!"

"No, Jaime," I said, my heart pounding a million miles an hour. I could see Jaime was as scared as I was. "Don't listen to them. Stay in the car! Stay in the car!"

"Get out of the fucking car!"

Jaime and I remained still.

"You fucking shitheads. I'm going to fuck you up!" The main shooter stormed over to Jaime's door and, much to my surprise, opened it. (I later discovered that all the ICE armored vehicles automatically unlocked when they were put into park.)

Jaime immediately grabbed the handle and slammed the door shut. "Lock the doors! Lock the doors!" he cried.

We frantically punched the lock buttons.

The shooter tried the door again. When it didn't open, he pointed the gun at Jaime. "Open the fucking door. Get the fuck out of the car right now. I'm going to kill you! Get out. Get out! *Get out!*"

"Do *not* get out, Jaime."

The man's metallic eyes met mine and sliced through me. He stepped back and shot four or five rounds into the door.

BOOM! BOOM! BOOM! BOOM! BOOM!

The armor deflected the shots, which otherwise would have blown us away.

Jaime, not knowing what to do, remained frozen with his hands raised in the air.

Waving furiously, I yelled to the shooter, "Come over here. Talk to me. Talk to me. We are Americans. We are U.S. Embassy employees. This is a diplomatic vehicle. You are confusing us with someone else. I have a diplomatic passport. Let me identify myself."

As the man walked toward us, I turned to find that two shooters had inserted the barrels of their guns into the vehicle, one right next to my head and the other six inches to the left. In the chaotic haste of button-pushing and door-locking, Jaime or I must have accidentally hit the window button, which was located right next to the lock button, and unrolled the window an inch or so—just enough space for a gun barrel.

I tried pushing my seat back so the guns weren't right next to my head, but it wouldn't budge. We had packed the equipment too tightly behind us. In desperation, I tried rolling up the window. The window ground against the hot metal. But I managed to push the barrels upward, so they were angled at the ceiling instead of at my temple. I held down the roll-up button for dear life, pushed my right shoulder hard against the doorpost, and moved as far away as possible from the line of fire—and then, unexpectedly, shots rang out. Bullets hit the ceiling, bouncing everywhere. The enclosed SUV amplified the gunfire blasts and the sound was deafening. I couldn't hear a thing except for the ringing in my ears. The explosions were so intense that I thought I might never be able to hear again. If, that is, I survived the next few minutes.

I could only watch helplessly as bullets hit Jaime. Had I been hit? Adrenaline had kicked in, and I wasn't sure.

"Go, go, go, Jaime! Hit the gas. Hit the gas. Go!"

"I'm shot! I'm hit!" Jaime moaned as bullets continued to rain on us.

The men pulled the guns out of the cab to reposition them, but I still held down the button, and the window rolled up as soon as they withdrew the barrels.

"Go. Go! Go!"

"I'm shot. I'm shot." Jaime held his side, blood gushing between his fingers.

I put the gear into drive with my left hand. "Hit the gas, Jaime!"

Jaime pressed on the gas pedal with what little strength he still had. I grasped his leg to push the pedal down harder. We crashed into one of the shooters' vehicles before veering left onto the road. Before long, Jaime slumped against the window, his hands slipping off the steering wheel. I grabbed for it, but the SUV swerved into the median. I tried desperately to pull us back on course, but the median was steep and rocky.

Soon, Jaime could no longer hold down the gas pedal, and we stopped.

"I'm going to die," he whispered.

I shook him, hard, trying to get him to keep his eyes open.

"You're not going to fucking die! Don't you do it, Jaime. Don't do it. I'm going to call for help."

His eyelids drooped. Blood was everywhere. Was it his ... or mine? I slapped him across the face, and his eyes shot open.

"I'm calling for help," I repeated, pressing the panic button on the dashboard. Every ICE vehicle came equipped with a panic button that alerted ICE Headquarters in Washington if we were in distress. Unfortunately, the GPS tracker on the panic button had been blinking red for months; something was malfunctioning. We'd informed our supervisors of the issue, but no one had addressed the problem. The button might not work, but it was worth a try. (It turns out that our distress call didn't reach headquarters until eight hours later.)

Out of the corner of my eye, I saw one of the SUVs fly past as though driving away. Instead, it pulled a U-turn, drove into the median, and faced us, its hood right next to ours. Two gunmen got out of the vehicle and walked toward us. One of the gunmen looked straight into my eyes. His expression was hard and cold, without a sign of compassion.

Both men walked calmly up to the bumper of our SUV and started shooting at the windshield over and over and over again. The front armored window stopped the bullets ... but I didn't know how much longer it would hold.

Chapter Seven

AFTERMATH IN THE LIFE OF THE AVILA FAMILY

I couldn't believe the assassins had returned.

"Blam! Blam! Blam!" They continued blasting away at the windshield.

Thankfully, it did not give way, though it had cracked so badly I could no longer see out of it.

Then, suddenly, the shooting stopped, and the shooters walked away. Car doors slammed. Through the side window, I watched, surprised, as both SUVs sped off.

I looked over at Jaime and saw that he was in bad shape. Blood was pouring out of wounds in his side and his leg. "Jaime! Jaime! Stay with me!" I shouted.

With shaky hands I began scrambling for my Nextel phone. No signal. Shit. I slammed it onto the floorboard in fury and reached for my backpack. It was stuck, wedged between the seat and the boxes. Shit. Shit. Shit! I managed to unzip it and pull out my GTIP phone.

I dialed the Embassy. Someone answered immediately, and I shouted into the phone:

"This is Victor Avila of ICE! We are shot! We are shot!

"We have been attacked and shot on the highway."

The operator asked me again for my name and location.

"My name is Victor Avila and I am an ICE special agent."

I urged him to call my boss, "He knows our location."

He urged me to stay on the line and I waited while he patched me through to the Regional Security Office. A voice I didn't recognize answered the phone—a woman with a heavy German accent—probably a floater temping for someone on vacation.

(Listen to Victor Avila's urgent phone call at www.LINK)

I didn't have time to think about why a random secretary was answering the emergency line. My words just bled out: "This is Victor Avila. We've been attacked on the highway. We've been shot! We need help. NOW!"

I heard a crash and assumed the secretary had dropped the phone.

I was right. That was exactly what she had done. She went running down the hall shouting, "Victor Avila's on the line. He's been shot! He's been shot?"

What she didn't know was that Claudia was working at the regional security office that day. She heard the woman shouting that I had been shot, and came running out of her office, demanding to know what had happened and what my condition was. But nobody knew.

Then Freddy's low voice boomed into my ear, "Victor, where are you?"

"I don't know. Somewhere south of San Luis Potosi. Send someone. Now!"

Marco's voice came on the line. I realized Freddy had put me on speaker phone when they started speaking simultaneously.

"Victor!" said Freddy, calling me to attention.

"Where is Jaime shot?" asked Marco. Before coming to work for ICE, he had been a firefighter and EMT

"In the side and in the leg. Shit. His leg's really bleeding—a lot."

"Put pressure on it. Put pressure on the leg!" they said in unison.

I propped the phone between my ear and my shoulder and pressed both hands on the wound. "Jaime! Jaime!"

Highway 57

Armored Suburban crime scene

Crime scene photo prior to me being
extracted and airlifted to hospital.

Agent Zapata and I being airlifted to
hospital in San Luis Potosi, Mexico

Operation Green Horizon

Working Narcotics on the border

Special Agent Zapata's funeral

Special Agent Jaime J. Zapata who
gave his life in service of our country.
EOW 2-15-2011

His eyes were open, but he wasn't blinking. He wasn't talking. "Jaime!" I yelled louder.

"Victor, check yourself. Are you shot?" Marco asked.

I obeyed. Blood and glass covered the cab, my chest hurt like hell and my shirt was drenched with blood. There was so much blood it was hard to tell where it was all coming from, but I feared I would bleed out right here on the highway. I was so concerned about my chest at the time that I didn't realize my left leg was swollen beyond recognition. "Oh shit! I think we're both going to die out here. Send someone right now!"

"Take off your belt and wrap it around the highest point of your swollen leg," said Marco, keeping his voice calm and steady.

I kept one hand on Jaime's leg, grateful the bleeding had slowed, and unbuckled my belt with the other.

Marco spoke again. "Victor. This is very important. Are you listening? Cinch your belt tight around the highest point of your leg."

"Yes, I got it."

"Okay. Keep pressure on it. I'm going to get someone out to you. Hold on."

I didn't want to hold on. I put Marco and Freddy on hold and called Roberto, my go-to-guy at the Mexican Federal Police. All of us at ICE had worked with him on a daily basis. He was one of the only people I could trust over there.

"Roberto, you have to send me help. I've been fucking shot. You need to send out a helicopter right now."

"Who is this?" he demanded, apparently confused by my demanding hysteria and lack of introduction. We mostly communicated through radio so he was not accustomed to hearing my voice on his landline.

I identified myself and explained the situation as quickly as I could. I could hear myself yelling and peppering my language with expletives, but I was too panic-stricken to even try reigning it in. My ears were still ringing. I could barely hear my own voice above the sheer whistling sound, so, although I didn't realize it at the time, I was shouting into the phone at the top of my lungs.

Roberto responded, "I'm going to get authorization to dispatch a helicopter. They're out to lunch right now, but we'll get it done."

While Roberto and I spoke, a federal police car passed by … slowly. Friendly? Corrupt? I didn't know.

"Roberto, they're here! The federal police — wait, they're driving away. Are you fucking kidding me? They're driving away!" The cruiser disappeared from view.

I sighed and stayed on the phone, switching from Freddie and Marco to Roberto and others, trying to get help. At some point, using all my might and strength, I managed to wiggle my backpack loose and pull out my guns. I then put one in my waistband – and held the other. If the shooters came back, I could at least fight. All the while, I kept shaking Jaime and yelling, "Jaime! Jaime! Stay with me!"

About twenty minutes after the cruiser disappeared, an ambulance arrived and stopped fifty or sixty yards away. Roberto hadn't ordered the ambulance, and I was immediately suspicious.

A man got out of the ambulance, walked toward us, and I pointed my gun at him. He wasn't dressed like an EMT, which made me even more suspicious.

He knocked on the door. "Open the door," he said.

"No, I don't know who you are."

Knowing that cartel members often pose as police officers, military members, EMTs, and other emergency responders, I couldn't trust anyone.

"Open the door," he said again.

"No. I won't."

Not until the shooters' trial in 2017 did I find out that this was a Los Zetas ambulance. In other words, the driver was another cartel member posing as an EMT, and he most likely would have killed me.

After he drove away, I turned my attention back to Jaime.

I called his name but got no response.

"Jaime! Jaimie!"

He was sitting straight up in the driver's seat. His mouth was slightly open and his eyes were open, too, staring straight ahead. I reached over and gently closed his eyes.

"Jaime," I whispered. "Help is on the way. You've got to hold on." Just an hour or so earlier he had been so excited about having a Subway sandwich for lunch. Now, his life was ebbing away. I felt so desperate. A combination of sadness and anger flooded through me. "For God's sake, hold on, Jaime!"

About ten minutes later, a state police officer drove up and got out of his car. He was dressed in jeans and a polo shirt, with a gun belt around his waist – the usual uniform of the state police. Still, I didn't trust him, so I kept my gun trained on him the entire time. He came around the back of the car, knocked on the door and asked me to open it.

"No! I don't know who you are."

He pulled on the door again. But when he saw it was locked, he turned around, hurried back to his car, and drove away.

I felt certain the cartel was trying to finish me off.

I called Roberto again and told him, "You need to give me a name for when your guys come. I need a name! Someone I can trust. Send someone I know I can trust."

"My guys are on the way. They're coming. You can answer to Commander Valdez. You can trust him. Just hang on."

Finally, the helicopter arrived, its whirring blades kicking up dust and drowning out all other sounds.

An officer came to the window and identified himself as Commander Valdez. I demanded to see his credentials. Only after he showed them to me was I willing to let him open the door. I made sure to hold onto my backpack, and I also kept a tight grip on my Blackberry.

Finally, the door was open, and the Mexican Federal Police were helping me out of the car.

"That's my bag and it doesn't leave my sight!" I told them.

"Okay. Okay."

They carried me shoulder to shoulder to the waiting chopper. "What about your partner?" one of them asked. "Is he dead?"

. "You go get him," I demanded. "I'm not leaving without him."

I kept searching the faces of the men who had come to my rescue. I wasn't sure that all of them were actually there to help me. Cartel thugs were everywhere in Mexico. One military guy stood out: he had that same metallic stare that had sliced through me before the shots rang out forty-five minutes earlier. A half-smoked cigar hung from his lips, and a smug look crossed his face when I glared at him.

They lifted me onto the gurney while I clutched the backpack to my chest. Within seconds, I was inside the helicopter, buckled into the front seat. I took a quick photo with my Blackberry. I intended to take another picture or even a video to fully document the scene. It was likely the story would be altered by the authorities, and I wanted evidence. But my hands shook so badly I accidentally turned off the phone and didn't get a second photo.

One of the EMTs shouted from our battered SUV. "Commander, I don't think this one is alive."

"We're taking Jaime with us! Don't you fucking leave him behind!" I stretched toward Jaime as if I intended to jump out of the helicopter and grab him myself. Someone restrained me.

"All right, all right, we're getting him," someone else said.

The EMT ducked into the cab of the SUV. "Wait, I think I feel a pulse!" he cried.

He dragged Jaime's limp body out of the bullet-riddled vehicle and onto a second gurney. Another emergency responder helped pull him into the helicopter cabin and laid him gently on the floor next to me. I touched Jaime's hand and silently prayed to Mother Mary and Joseph that he'd survive.

With the pilot, a police officer, Jaime, and me on board, the ground fell away beneath us, the helicopter lifting and pulling us higher and higher into the clear blue sky. I stayed on the phone the entire time, talking to the commander in Mexico City and begging him to send reinforcements, certain we would be killed as soon as we landed. The commander promised to send someone who could be trusted. First, he had to find that someone.

Eight minutes later we landed on the heliport at *Hospital de la Salud*. Instead of feeling safe, I was even more petrified. The town was overrun by the Zetas cartel, and the cartels were famous for finishing off their intended victims in the hospital if an ambush had failed or their target had survived. They went so far as to murder survivors who dared attend the funerals of victims they had succeeded in killing. It was not unusual for those who had been shot to cross the border into El Paso hoping to make it to a hospital for treatment.

Jaime and I may have made it to the hospital, but danger still surrounded us.

Upon landing, I secured my backpack between my legs, determined to keep it with me. I knew that if the authorities found the guns I was carrying, they would take them away from me. And I might need them.

Hospital personnel waited, ready to spring into action. They wheeled me to the trauma center, and from there to a bed in a room with big lights but no windows. I announced that I would keep my phone—and my backpack—with me at all times. In response they cut off my clothes and examined my wounds. In addition to being shot in my side and leg, I had sustained multiple injuries from embedded shrapnel. I stayed on the phone with the federal police throughout the examination. I felt the throbbing pain, yet I was numb with adrenaline.

I refused all pain medication. I couldn't afford to be sedated or have my senses dulled. My life was on the line. I had survived their bullets, so far, but they could easily kill me with medication. I would take no chances. The doctor who tended to me did not take the 5 millimeter bullet out of my leg because of its precarious position near the femoral artery. Every person who walked into my room was suspect. I had never felt panic-stricken alertness until then.

————

About an hour later—though it seemed much longer—a reinforcement of police officers arrived, armed in SWAT-type gear.

"This building is now secure. No one is getting in. No one is going to hurt you," an officer announced.

For the first time in hours, I relaxed ... a little. Frustration welled and I shouted to everyone within earshot, "I'm an American and my name is Victor Avila. I'm an ICE Special Agent. I work for the U.S. Embassy."

The doctors and nurses glanced at each other. Their eyes widened, but they kept working as they absorbed this new information. They had an international incident on their hands. I wasn't just another officer; I was an American—and I worked for the U.S. government. While they didn't change their treatment of me, I could see my disclosure had made an impact. Once the hospital staff realized that Jaime and I were Americans, everything changed. More Federales poured into the hospital to make sure we were safe. They realized Mexico would be in the glare of the world's spotlight, and they knew they needed to respond properly.

As for me, I felt like such a foreigner. Even being of Mexican descent, I knew I didn't belong there. I was an American, and I wanted to go home. Mexico was my family's country of origin, but I felt like I might as well be in China, or any other country that was completely foreign to me.

Hospital personnel were still tending to my wounds when another doctor approached. Dread flooded my heart when I saw his serious expression.

"I'm sorry to tell you, your friend has expired," he said in Spanish, using the word *expiró*.

Expired. Not died. Not passed away. Not even "We lost him." *Expired*.

I didn't appreciate the doctor using the term. Jaime wasn't a carton of milk.

"Please treat him with dignity and respect," I said, my voice choking.

"We will, sir."

Jaime was gone. A young man with a family who loved him and a fiancée he had planned a life with … gone. It made no sense. He had been my partner for only a day, but the loss to me was devastating. How much harder would it be for his loved ones? I didn't want to think about it.

They wheeled me from one room to another for treatment and tests, my backpack still in my possession. At one point they moved me to a higher floor for even greater security.

A couple of hours had passed when the building began to shake and the windows rattled. The helicopter we had flown in on earlier still occupied the heliport, forcing the arriving Blackhawk to land in the green area next to the hospital.

Before long, an officer stood at my bedside. My nerves jangled when I recognized him as being second in command of the entire Mexican federal police force. I had actually had a lunch meeting with him and a Mexican congresswoman a few months earlier to discuss the problem of human trafficking.

His demeanor stern, his dark eyes reflecting no concern for my condition, the commander introduced himself and thrust his cell phone in front of my face. On screen was a picture of a blue Suburban. "Victor, a terrible mistake has been made. This car belongs to the local chief of police. The shooters apparently thought they were shooting at him."

I looked at the photo of a blue Suburban and shook my head. There was some resemblance, but not too much. For one thing, the vehicle Jaime and I were riding in was clearly armored. For another thing, it had diplomatic plates. Plus, I was sure that the killers had heard me shouting that we were on a diplomatic mission – a fact they later verified in their trial. "That's not the Suburban we were driving," I said flatly.

He nodded and sighed. "Yes, we know that now. It is a regret-table—but understandable—error."

So that was his game. He was trying to avoid any repercussions on the part of the United States by convincing us that there had not been a deliberate attack on anyone from our government. But I knew better.

"Don't you remember me?" I asked, looking directly into his face.

His cold eyes narrowed and considered me.

"We had lunch a few months ago. Do you remember?"

Instantly, the color seemed to drain from his face. Without a word, he turned on his heel and left.

He had remembered.

———

All this time my adrenaline had been surging, sending my heart rate and blood pressure through the roof. Medical staff worked frantically to bring my vitals down, as I was in danger of having a heart attack. But strangely enough, I didn't feel a bit of pain.

I finally managed to contact Claudia to reassure her I was alive and that the doctors were taking good care of me. I must admit I have no idea what I said to her, but she related to me that she had been at the embassy when the receptionist had answered my call. Not knowing what to do, the temp had run down the hall yelling, "Victor Avila's been shot!" Claudia, a mere five feet away, came out of her office as fast as lightning.

"What did you say? Victor Avila? That's my husband!"

Claudia spared me all the heartache of the chaos that followed after my call into the RSO's office that fateful afternoon. It was much later when she recounted in graphic detail what my family had endured for 48 hours before we were reunited in El Paso.

News stations had already begun broadcasting stories of the attack, and I panicked. Like me, my dad is a news junkie and spent hours watching television. What if my parents saw the news-casts and thought I was dead? At least one station had mistakenly reported the name of the murdered federal agent as a combination of my and Jaime's names.

I immediately called a friend in El Paso who knew where my parents lived. I urged him to get to them as fast as he could and to call me as soon as he got there.

"Lights and sirens!" I said. "Go now. Tell them I'm alive before they see the news!"

"On my way, Victor."

I learned later that my parents were indeed listening to the news and believed the fallen agent to be me. Right at that moment, the doorbell rang, and they were convinced someone had come to break the bad news to them. My dad almost collapsed when he opened the door and saw my friend.

"No, no! He's alive! Victor's alive." He caught my dad in his arms.

"I don't believe you...I don't believe you."

My friend called me so my parents could hear my voice.

"I'm okay. I just wanted you to hear it directly from me," I assured them. "I'll call you soon."

After news of the shooting hit the airwaves, it seemed like everyone I knew in Mexico and the United States called me. The doctor again wanted to give me medication, but I refused. Soon pain began seeping in, and I realized—of all things—my left index finger hurt! When the assassins had been firing into the Suburban, I had instinctively grabbed the muzzle of a handgun in an attempt to push it away and had burned my finger. It struck me as almost funny. I had been shot three times, my leg had swollen like a huge balloon, and I sustained other wounds from shrapnel, yet I noticed a burned finger.

The shooting had taken place about 2:15 in the afternoon, but it wasn't until around 7 or 8 p.m. that the first American arrived. He was a colleague who had worked with me at various times during my tenure in Mexico. As soon as he heard about the shooting, he was sent to the hospital. He didn't know who had been attacked, but he was aware that Jaime and I were in the area, so he was afraid we might be involved.

It was such a relief for me to see a friendly and familiar face. Soon after, many more friends and co-workers arrived: ICE special agents, Secret Service Special Agents, DEA Special Agents, FBI Agents and officers from the U.S. Marshal's service. I saw the concern and anguish in their eyes and I drew strength from their presence.

Early the next morning, about 2:30, a DEA airplane arrived to transport me to Houston. I have only flashes of memories of that trip. I remember being wheeled onto the airplane at the crack of dawn. . .being loaded onto an ambulance. . .being surrounded by lots of police. . .a motorcade. . .another ambulance…and finally my arrival at the trauma center.

My doctor there told me that the medical staff in Mexico had done a meticulous job. "You were in good hands," he said. He also agreed with their decision to leave the bullet in my leg. And it's still there.

———

After my time in Houston, a plane provided by Customs & Border Protection transported me home to El Paso. I couldn't wait to see my family. Marco escorted Claudia and the children out of Mexico and came with them to meet me. He was a welcome sight. I remember how he cried as we hugged each other. After what I had been through, I longed to be with people who cared about me. How wonderful it felt to see the compassion in friendly eyes.

I don't remember many details about my reunion with Claudia and the kids. It took place in an El Paso hangar, and they were transported to Texas in a CBP plane from Toluca, Mexico. They ran toward me and surrounded my wheelchair, and we clung to each other amid sobs, disbelief that such a thing had happened, and relief that we had come through and were together again.

I wore hospital scrubs, as my clothes had been cut off by hospital personnel in Mexico. Thank heaven my father brought me sweatpants and a sweatshirt!

We spent the next few days at my parents' home, protected 24/7 by the El Paso HSI Special Response Team (SRT). Mom and Dad have lived in the same house—and had the same phone number—for over forty years, so the place was very familiar and comforting to me. But before long, I felt like I was living in a circus. The phone rang constantly. Family and friends poured in and out ... day and night. Mom insisted on feeding the entire SRT team. The media and curiosity seekers camped out in droves, but were kept away from our door by the SRT. The FBI came to see me. So did the DEA and members of the Secret Service – and those are just the tip of the iceberg.

I couldn't handle all the turmoil in addition to the aftermath of the ordeal on Highway 57. Small things became big deals. My hair had grown so much, and one day, I simply couldn't stand it any longer.

"I have to cut my hair. I *need* to cut my hair," I told Claudia. And I needed it cut right then. I called my barber in El Paso, and he told me to come on over. I went ... and a whole caravan of people went with me.

Two days after the assault, a counselor from El Paso met with us at home. After speaking with Victor Emilio and Sofia, she disclosed her concerns to Claudia and me.

"Your kids know more than you think," she began. "They feel left out." She encouraged us to talk openly about what had happened, to include our children.

We had tried to protect them from trauma, from knowing someone had tried to kill their dad. Instead, for two days they had felt abandoned to an extent. Mom and Dad were dealing with something huge and scary … and they had been excluded.

After the counselor left, we sat down together and explained the events to the kids and, from then on, made a conscious effort to include them. They were going through this, too.

Our family dynamic has been different ever since. The counselor's advice didn't change the way we parent, but it did impact the way Claudia and I interact with our children. As a result, our relationship has opened up, and we are a much closer family. We discuss family matters, unlike the way I was brought up, and include the entire family. Everyone's input and opinions are included whenever possible.

———

I still had no clothes with me, and so after the barber, Claudia and another convoy headed to Dillard's to buy a suit for Jaime's funeral.

To accommodate the thousands of people attending, Jaime's funeral was held in a convention center in Brownsville. When we arrived, I was asked if I would meet Jaime's parents. Of course, I agreed, and Claudia and I followed the attendant to a room set aside for the family. I expected Jaime's parents, his brothers, and perhaps his fiancée. Met by an audible gasp when we entered the room, I was stunned to come face to face with about fifty people.

"There's Victor Avila!"

"He's here!"

All eyes were on me, but no one approached, giving me time to get to my feet and anchor crutches under my arms. Then

Jaime's mother rushed me, throwing her arms around my neck and insisting I tell her everything.

I could only say, "I'm sorry for the loss of your son. I will tell you everything when the time is right. I'll share everything I know. You'll get everything from me ... everything Jaime and I talked about ... everything."

Questions bombarded me left and right and, overwhelmed, I started crying. I couldn't deal with all the questions. I couldn't handle the outpouring of their grief. I could barely manage my own. I hadn't expected the panic that overwhelmed me, and I had to get out. With Claudia's help, I collapsed into the wheelchair and hurried from the room amid apologies to the family. There would be plenty of time later to talk through the tragic events of that day.

Chapter Eight

THE HERO NOBODY WANTED

M y recovery was slow and painful.
But I knew that it was only by the grace of God that I was alive, while Jaime was dead and lying in a grave. I tried not to think too much about it, but when I did I felt guilty. Survivor's remorse was foreign to me. There was no reason why I had been chosen to live while Jaime's life had been taken from him. And yet, I knew that my children needed me, and Claudia needed me – so perhaps it was for their sake that I had been spared.

As I recovered from the physical and emotional wounds caused by the armed attack, I was honored at a number of dinners and banquets where I was asked to tell my story and was applauded as a true American hero. But while many good things were said about me, the truth was that nobody seemed to want me around.

The consensus was that I couldn't go back to Mexico City because my life would be in immediate danger. I knew that was true. The Los Zetas Cartel had thousands of foot soldiers throughout the country of Mexico, and any one of them would be happy to finish me off.

Meanwhile, in the aftermath of the shooting, other organizations were hailing me as a hero. So were many of the people in ICE whom I considered to be my brothers and sisters. But as far as the top brass was concerned, they just wanted me to go away. I didn't want any favors. I wasn't a whiner or a complainer, nor did I go around with a victim attitude. I just wanted an opportunity to get the physical rehab I needed, and then get back to work so I could show what I could do. Yes, I had been through tremendous terror and trauma. I was still on crutches, and it was going to take some time and rehabilitation services before I was back in top form. But that didn't mean I was damaged goods. I knew I still had what it takes.

After Jaime's funeral, I was told that I was to be relocated to Washington, D.C. and would be able to rehab there. Within a few days of hearing this, we were moved into a hotel in Falls Church, Virginia. We were told that the first two weeks of our rent was provided. After that, I wasn't sure what we were going to do. We were on our own.

We didn't know it, but we were about to embark on one of the loneliest, most frustrating times of our life together. Claudia was given one-hour notice to pack when they extracted my family from Mexico City on the night of the attack. Most of what we owned was still in our place in Mexico City, so we called some friends to go into our apartment, pick up whatever items they thought we needed most and ship them to us. Another problem was that it was February, and the weather in Washington was bitterly cold, with snow or cold rain falling just about every day. In Mexico City, the temperature this time of year averaged 72 degrees, so none of us had boots or other clothing to keep us warm in the Washington winter.

When we tried to enroll our kids in school, the administrators would not accept the Residence Inn as an official address. They required a house or apartment in the city before Sofia and Victor would be allowed to attend school. It didn't seem fair to me, especially given our circumstances – but we were all tangled up in red tape and nobody seemed willing to help us cut through it. My kids were at risk of losing school credit, Claudia had lost her job at the embassy and was preoccupied with putting together a makeshift home in a different city, and I was confined to crutches, feeling responsible for this chaos.

Somehow, we needed to find a house, move in, buy appropriate clothing, get the children's medical appointments and all documentation in order, buy school supplies, enroll them in school, attend my medical appointments — and, meanwhile, I was moving like a guy who had been shot to pieces and had an injured shoulder and a big bullet hole in his leg. I was trying to get used to walking on crutches after weeks in a wheelchair, and I wasn't setting any land-speed records. It took me five minutes just to get out of the car, and there was quite a bit of pain involved.

At first, it seemed like we were never going to find a house or apartment that would work with us. Then, somehow, I happened upon an apartment building where the manager seemed sympathetic to us because she worked with a lot of families who were associated with the state department. I told her I didn't know how long we were going to be there – six months, a year, two years – I had no idea. She was very accommodating, and whereas they usually asked for a year's lease, she would make an exception, and we could pay on a month-to-month basis.

Finally, someone was willing to work with us. I was really happy about that, until I went back to the ICE office and talked to the accounts payable clerk there, who was responsible for processing my housing payment. When I informed her of our new address, she just shook her head and said, "It's not on my list."

"What do you mean?" I asked.

"I can't pay for it, because it's not on my list."

I didn't understand. "You were paying for our housing in Mexico City. Why can't you stop paying for that and start paying for the apartment here, instead."

She glared at me, "Because we don't have a *funding mechanism*."

That wasn't the last time I was to hear those words, which I have come to hate with a passion. Whenever I think about all of the thousands of dollars I've had to spend out of my own pocket because I was shot – on duty – I always remember that it's because there is "no funding mechanism."

I had reached the end of my rope. I must have been a pitiful sight, leaning on my crutches, trying to keep my emotions under control. I could feel the burning in my throat and wanted to lash out. However, I turned around and tried to "storm" out of there. But it's awfully hard to do that when you can't walk without crutches.

There were so many reasons why our stint in D.C. was such a trying time for Claudia and me. After my injury, she became unemployed and had to take care of me. I found out pretty quick that I was living off one paycheck instead of two. And believe me, the cost of living in Washington D.C. is quite a bit higher than it was in Mexico City.

After the cartel members were arrested and went on trial for Jaime's murder and my attempted murder, as a victim of a crime, I had to write a Victim Impact Statement. This document shows the total out of pocket expenses incurred due to the attack. Of course, I thought this was rather funny because – let's face it – I knew there was no way those murderers would pay back the financial distress they caused me. Still, when we figured out how much money we had spent because of my injuries, the total came to over $200,000! Out of our pockets.

During our time in Mexico, Claudia and I agreed to save as much money as we could. Other than the vacation trip to the beach I mentioned earlier, we lived a pretty frugal existence. By the time of the shooting, we had put $40,000 in our savings account. Now it was gone, and I had spent a good deal of the money from my 401K.

And now, they were basically telling me, "Good luck, kid. You're on your own."

As it turned out, after much back-and-forth discussion, within a week or two I was informed that my housing would be paid for after all. I was exhausted from fighting for everything!

For example, as we moved into our new apartment, we purchased pantry staples, cleaning supplies, linens, hygiene products, school supplies, jackets, coats, boots, winter clothing, etc. Between Wal-Mart, Safeway, and Marshalls we spent a small fortune. My agency never offered to assist with any costs. I sometimes tell people, imagine if you left your house one morning, and then discovered you could not return. What if you suddenly found yourself in another part of the country and had taken nothing with you. What would you need? Everything! A toothbrush. A pillow. Soap. Sheets and towels. Kitchen utensils. The list goes on and on – and your bill could run into thousands of dollars very fast, especially if you were buying for a family of four.

We weren't the only ones who were lost and lonely in Virginia. Our kids were miserable, too. I vividly remember hearing Sofia crying softly in bed one night. I came into her room and asked what was the matter. With a tearful face, she told me, "Daddy, I don't like to eat by myself. I have no friends and I don't want to go back to school." She missed everything we left behind abruptly in Mexico and that broke my heart. This was a girl who never had any trouble making friends. For some reason, Northern Virginia was not working for us.

All this time, I was being besieged for interviews. I received many phone calls and emails from newspapers, magazines and TV shows wanting me to tell them what had happened to Jaime and me on Highway 57. I was basically ordered not to respond to any of those requests, most probably because the government knew I'd be getting questions I couldn't answer without making my bosses look inept. Questions like, "What were you doing out there on a road that the State Department had declared to be dangerous and off-limits to all embassy employees?" "Did you express your fears to your bosses?" And so on. I kept my mouth shut because I was a loyal agent. If I had it to do all over again, I wouldn't handle things the same way.

———

Just when I'd reached the point that I wasn't sure I could take another month in Washington, a friend called me and told me he heard there was an opening for an assistant Attachè in the ICE Office at the U.S. Embassy in Madrid.

"Thanks for letting me know," I told him, "but I don't think that's the place for me."

"Why not?" he wanted to know.

"I'm not the kind of guy they're looking for."

"But you'd be really good at it," he protested.

I told him I appreciated his faith in me. "But you know who gets those jobs in Madrid, Copenhagen, London, places like that."

"Who?"

"People who are connected, who have friends in high places."

My friend understood what I was saying, but told me, "It won't hurt you to look into it."

I wasn't sure, at first, that I wanted to move out of the country. But the more I thought about it, the better it sounded to me. Maybe it was just what I needed.

I knew that the director of the office in Washington had spent five years in Madrid when he was a younger man, so I decided to go tell him I was interested in the job.

I stepped into his office late one afternoon and told him, "I hear the Madrid office has an opening."

He nodded, "Yes it does. Are you interested?"

"I am," I said. "And you're going to send me and my family there."

I hadn't meant for it to come out like an order, but that's what happened.

"You really want it?"

"I do," I said. "We really have to get out of here."

To my surprise, he looked almost pleased that I had asked about transferring to Spain. But on the other hand, he was probably delighted by the thought of getting rid of me. "Well, let me see what I can do."

A few days later, word came down that the job was mine. I would be spending the next three years in Spain! I'm pretty sure that the position had already been promised to someone else. But I had seniority, so they had to bump him – whoever he was – and give the position to me. I don't have any proof that this is so. But it makes sense to me based on what happened to me during the rest of my career.

In a lot of ways, I enjoyed life in Madrid. The pace was much slower than it had been in Mexico, and that was nice, even though I'm a guy who likes to keep busy. It was a true diplomatic post. I wore a suit and tie to work and my days were full of meetings and paperwork instead of being out on the street chasing criminals and at risk of my life. But even here, there was a stigma attached to me. Much to my displeasure, I was always labeled as "the guy who got shot." Or, "the guy who survived the shootout."

Plus, there were some other ways Spain didn't turn out to be the new start I was hoping for. As much as I tried to fit in, and just be "one of the guys," it seemed that nobody wanted to reciprocate. Claudia and I were shunned by the other ICE agents and their wives, and never felt included in the embassy community. Other than that, we loved being in Spain. I was committed to ensuring my family and I made the best of our stay in Europe, despite being ostracized by my own agency. Claudia and I both enjoyed the fact that nobody knew who we were. Our anonymity was extremely therapeutic, and our kids were much happier than they'd been in Virginia. However, my bosses and co-workers were not at all welcoming. Quite the contrary. They were all very dismissive individuals. Claudia and I are both friendly, outgoing people, yet we spent Thanksgiving by ourselves. No invitations, much less a slice of pie and a cup of coffee.

I told Claudia that we shouldn't worry about things like that – that we were blessed to be a complete family, and would make the best of our stay in this beautiful country. And we did. But it hurt to be treated like outsiders.

———

After several months in Spain, I began falling apart emotionally. I was in weekly counseling – which I paid for out of my own pocket – but I was tumbling deeper into Post Traumatic Stress Disorder (PTSD). I expected that whatever mental or emotional damage I had suffered would get better over time – not worse. But instead, I jumped whenever there was a loud noise, I was having night terrors, and had trouble focusing on simple daily tasks. Sometimes, doing the smallest thing seemed like a major burden to me, and I just wanted to stay in the house and hide at night. When I left Washington, D.C, I told all my doctors that I was well and ready to go back to work. I was sure that I had put the shooting behind me for good. All the doctors agreed, except my counselor, who told me, "Post Traumatic Stress Disorder is a strange thing. You never know when it will rear its ugly head and start causing trouble. So, yes, I'll release you. But I'm going to do

it with the caveat that I'm here to help if and when you need me."
She was right. PTSD had a grip on me and I couldn't get free. My
heart pounded constantly. I couldn't catch my breath or shake off
the feelings of dread. There were many other issues that caused
me a great deal of physical and emotional pain.

Some people think, "You got shot, so get over it." But they
don't understand the long-lasting impact – both physical and
mental – that comes from being attacked in the line of duty. For
instance, I undergo regular, painful treatments for hyperhidrosis—
abnormally excessive sweating. My palms and underarms don't
just grow damp; they drip. Regardless of the temperature, I soak
through undershirt, dress shirt, and suit coat. In addition to dis-
rupting normal activities, this disorder not only stains my clothes
but causes me great embarrassment and impairs business and
social interactions.

Every three or four months, I'm given Botox injections in my
hands and underarms. The treatment is agonizing, but the hyperhidrosis is finally lessening somewhat. There are enough reminders
of that day on Highway 57. Another symptom that I don't have
to worry about.

My reason in doing this is not to show you how much I have
suffered – but rather, as a salute to all the men and women in
law enforcement and our military who have put their lives on the
line to uphold the law and protect our homeland, in some cases,
suffered terribly because of it. We owe them all a huge debt of
gratitude!

Serving in law enforcement has always been demanding and
difficult, and it is even more stressful today. Over the last few
years, the stress has become so intense and profound that many
officers are retiring early, recruitment has fallen off, and even
worse, the suicide rate has increased dramatically. A nonprofit
organization called Blue H.E.L.P. says that 228 police officers
committed suicide in 2018, up from 172 the year before – and
that was before 2020 brought further disrespect for law enforcement, calls for defunding the police, and vilification of all men and
women in uniform for the egregious actions of a few.

I know all too well what this kind of stress bears – PTSD, panic attacks, insomnia, overwhelming anxiety, hyperhidrosis and much more. Law enforcement agencies of all levels must put more of an emphasis on the mental wellness of their agents and officers. It's so important to do everything we can to support them and keep them strong in body and mind. Where would we be without the men and women who serve us as law enforcement officers? I hate to think about it. Law enforcement is a calling. It takes a special person to put his or her life on the line every day to shield us from harm. Let's do what we can to let them know how much we appreciate it.

As for me, the mere act of getting out of bed in the morning was becoming more and more difficult. And then one day, I couldn't get up at all. I tried to sit up and put my feet on the floor, but my legs wouldn't cooperate. The room wasn't exactly spinning, but I felt like I was on a ship, rolling back and forth. And, I had a powerful sensation of dread and doom. The only way I can describe is that it felt like the devil was in the room with me.

In other words, I felt absolutely horrible and knew I couldn't.

Staying home was not at all easy for me. I wanted to be working – to take care of my family. When I was growing up, I was one of those kids who never missed a day of school. Early in my school years I began winning awards for perfect attendance, and I kept that up through my senior year in high school. Yes, there were days when I was miserably sick and should have stayed home, but I went to school anyway. When I grew up and started my career, I did the same thing. I just didn't take sick days, and I was proud of it. For me to stay home was a really big deal.

Now, I had been sick during our time in Virginia, but that was all physical. For several hours after the shooting, I didn't feel any pain at all – except the constant loud ringing in my ears that I thought would never go away. But when the pain hit, it hit with a vengeance. My back ached, my shoulder throbbed, my legs buckled when I tried to walk. It seemed to me that every inch of my body was in pain.

But what happened to me in Spain was far worse than anything I had ever experienced before. When your body hurts, you have hope that it's going to get better. But when your soul is damaged and hurting, you feel like you're never, ever going to get better. In March of 2012, I started losing my hair. I slept fitfully, if at all. I perspired constantly. I could be in a room where the temperature was set at 70 degrees, and sweat would be running down my face, and my shirt would be soaked. And my jaw hurt because I was always clenching my teeth.

On the day when I finally hit bottom, I called my boss and told him I couldn't make it into the office that day.

"Sure," he said. "Take it easy and feel better."

Although I didn't want to tell him right then and there, I knew that a day of bed-rest wasn't going to restore me to normal. Following the medical advice from my therapist, I scheduled a meeting to ask for an extended period of time off.

They finally agreed to give me 30 days.

"I don't think 30 days is going to be long enough," I said. "I need more time." My doctor had told me, "I don't know how much time you need, but it will be several months. Maybe years."

"No," I was told. "That's just not possible."

I asked if I could go on worker's compensation, but was again told that was impossible.

"Why not?"

"Because you're working overseas. You have to be working in the United States in order to take worker's compensation."

I didn't find out until years later that this was totally untrue.

As it turned out, I did get the time I needed, but only because of my tendency not to take days off. It turned out that I had accumulated more than 1,000 hours of unused sick days and vacation, and I used it all up to get the intensive therapy and rest I needed. Those were difficult days for Claudia and me. I know there were times when she feared I was never going to get better, and I felt terribly guilty because I wondered if she was disappointed that I wasn't the man she had fallen in love with and married. But as much as the therapy I went through helped me, I'm certain that her hugs, kisses, and words of love and encouragement helped me even more.

On my 40th birthday, in August of 2012, my family and I flew to Puerto Rico where an award was being presented to me from the ICE Hispanic Agents Association.

But just as Claudia and I sat down at our table for the luncheon ceremony, we were approached by James Dinkins, who was the head of Homeland Security Investigations for ICE. Dinkins, a wide-built tall man, squatted down between us and said, "The U.S. Ambassador wants you out of Spain." What? I was completely caught off guard and had no idea how to react. I had never even met the ambassador. The only one I knew in his office was the Deputy Chief of Mission, who was second in command.

I felt like I'd been slapped across the face. For one thing, his timing was terrible. I was about to receive an important award – and now every bit of joy had been drained out of the occasion. For another, we were supposed to be in Spain for 36 months, but had been there only slightly over half this time. What about security for me and my family? Didn't we need to relocate somewhere the cartels weren't active? Instead, I was assured we would be safe anywhere we chose. Security wasn't an issue. Absolutely no effort was made to advise me or to protect my family.

When we got back to Madrid, I decided to call the Deputy Chief of Mission in the ambassador's office and ask why his boss wanted me to be replaced. There was silence for a moment or two, and then he asked, "Are you serious? Who told you that?"

When I responded, he said, "Why would the ambassador want you out? That's ridiculous."

"Well, that's what I was told."

"I guarantee you, it's not true. To be honest with you, I doubt if the ambassador even knows your name. "

"There's no reason he should," I agreed.

"I swear, Victor. Somebody's lying to you. If the ambassador had a problem with you, I'd know about it."

This whole thing was becoming more and more mysterious. But whatever the reason may have been, my days in Madrid were coming to an end. Over the next few weeks, my bosses pestered me constantly. "Where do you want to go Victor?" "You know you've got to pick a place?" "You'd better hurry up and choose?"

I tried to fight it, for a while, but on October 15, 2012, I received a 3R letter, which is usually sent to agents who commit an egregious violation of policy, are charged with a crime, or have shown that they have lost their integrity. Everybody knew that I was an honest, straight-shooting guy. And as far as I could see, the only thing I'd done wrong was getting shot. Still, the letter said that I had 90 days to get out of Spain. My options were to resign, retire or relocate. If I didn't choose, the decision would be made for me. Obviously, my days in Spain had come to an end.

Before making a decision about where to go next, I contacted friends at the FBI and DEA for intel on where the cartels were active and was told to steer clear of Dallas and Atlanta.

How about San Antonio? I was familiar with the place, having served there as a Federal Probation Officer. It was still in Texas, so it was close enough for Claudia and me to see our families. It was busy, so I knew there would be plenty for me to do there. And, it would be safer than El Paso, since the border with Mexico is over 140 miles away. In other words, it was unlikely that someone could sneak into San Antonio, attack me or my family, and then slip quickly back across the border.

I was shocked and dismayed when word came back that the Special Agent in Charge in San Antonio didn't want me in her city. The official explanation was that there was no position for me. But it seemed clear to me that she was really afraid of having me in her office. She didn't really know what to do with me, and thought that, because I had been shot by the Zetas cartel, I might be a distraction and a liability. Unfortunately, that attitude was not unique to San Antonio.

I really couldn't figure it out. I had always been a hard-working, honest agent with an exemplary record.

What's more, the fact that I was nearly killed didn't have anything to do with recklessness on my part. I had tried to tell my supervisors that they were sending Jaime and me into harm's way, but they wouldn't listen to me. Nothing that happened to us on Highway 57 was my fault or Jaime's fault.

After San Antonio said no, I suggested Austin and Flagstaff, but was told that neither of those cities was a suitable match for me. Three cities. Three denials. My choices finally boiled down to Tampa or Denver. We chose Denver.

Once the decision was made, I was told to report to Denver on December 23. I immediately protested. I was not going to move my family to a new location—where we knew no one—and check into a hotel two days before Christmas. That seemed so insensitive and intentional. After much discussion, they finally agreed to January 20 as our arrival date.

Though it was a bit of a reprieve, Claudia was not pleased. When James Dinkins visited the Madrid office, Claudia and I, along with several other agents, went to dinner. Claudia spoke with Dinkins about the situation. We had been through similar moves twice in quick succession—leaving Mexico City after the shooting and then the move to Madrid from Washington, D.C. She didn't want to take the kids out of school and put them through the ordeal of transitioning in the middle of the year—again. She begged him, with a pleading voice, to allow us to stay in Madrid a few more months.

Dinkins was coldly unsympathetic and denied the request on the spot. It broke my heart to see my wife so distraught, and I urged her not to give him the satisfaction of seeing her cry. But she was so angry—so upset, she couldn't hold back the tears.

Despite the orders to arrive in Denver by January 20, I still had not received my orders—or any paperwork—by the middle of December. I called the office several times only to be told the paperwork hadn't even been initiated. How was I supposed to get my family to Denver in a month without official orders?

One day I called my office to inquire about the paperwork for my move. I had always dealt with Permanent Change Station (PCS) before, but now I was told that I was going through "The Workforce Commission." "The what?" I had never heard of this group before. What was going on? I didn't have any orders.

I learned later that the Workforce Commission deals with agents that have been issued 3R letters. In other words, they handle agents who have committed an egregious offense in some way and are being transferred as punishment.

When I called to find out what had happened, I immediately noticed a disrespectful attitude on the other end of the phone. The woman talked to me as though I had done something wrong. When I questioned her about her attitude, she asked if I expected to be respected after what I had done. I had no idea what she was talking about and told her so. Whatever it was, our association was anything but smooth and pleasant.

I had to fight to maintain my composure, and I'm not sure I succeeded very well. On top of that bit of mystery, trying to move from one country to another in less than thirty days—in the middle of the Christmas season—was extremely stressful. I still don't know how we pulled it off, but we made it to Denver as directed. When I reported to the office, I was issued a government car and informed that my new position would be that of program manager. I had no idea what that entailed. The car was a Chevrolet Avalanche, same year and same color as the Suburban that we were ambushed in. They are the exact same vehicle except for the cargo area. As I drove out, I had a flashback of the attack.

I also knew I was still dealing with PTSD, so I reapplied for workers comp, which was approved and reinstated in April 2013. I again underwent treatment—both physical and psychological. During that time, I dealt with shoulder surgery and debilitating back spasms, among other issues.

———

It was when I lived in Denver that I thought of Nick Martin, a correspondent for Sky News in the United Kingdom, who I had met in Mexico City. Martin and his crew had followed me as I worked a human trafficking case. He won an award for the story, and we had kept in touch. I decided to reach out to Nick and told him what had happened and what I wanted to do. Nick and his producer were in Denver a week later, and we began working on the documentary "Agent Down" (now available on YouTube).

After the shooting on Highway 57, I had wanted to return to my family's old apartment in Mexico City to see what was still there, as a lot of things had been stolen or were missing. Not only were there belongings to be packed and shipped, but I also needed closure. I wanted to spend some time back where we had lived so I could anchor myself and then move forward. Three times I had pleaded to be allowed to return. Three times I was denied. [About eight months after the ambush, Claudia had returned to pack and store our possessions until everything could be shipped to Madrid.]

Through Nick Martin's contacts, flights and armored-car security details were arranged. Interviews were conducted and reenactments taped.

Nick obtained documents through his media contacts, and we discovered that the ATF had identified the weapons traffickers months before the shooting, but had decided against arresting them. After the ambush, ATF waited a week before picking up the shooters. The agency retraced their steps and doctored the paperwork. Reports were written in February 2011 but backdated to October 2010, contributing to the cover up.

After wrapping up production in Mexico, we flew to Brownsville and met with Jaime's family to conclude the story. I was well pleased with the end result and hoped it would lead to at least a bit of justice for me and my family.

Chapter Nine

NO QUESTIONS ASKED

On May 1, 2015, I took a medical retirement. I still didn't know what I had done that had caused me to fall into disfavor with "the powers that be," but I felt I had no other choice.

I had survived a violent attack, and my agency was not equipped to deal with the aftermath. Yes, I know how sarcastic that sounds. But it's also the only way I know to explain how I was treated by the agency I had devoted my life to. I had always been a very loyal employee, I expected the agency to back me up.

But the truth was that, for all intents and purposes, I lost my job the day I was shot. I was never going to have the privilege of being a Special Agent again. Of course, there was a different man in the White House then, and a different attorney general. If the shooting had happened today, I think it would have all turned out differently.

Occasionally, after we moved to Denver, I'd bump into agents I hadn't seen since the shooting, and they would joke and basically ask the same thing.

"Hey, Victor! What's going on? Are you the head of an office now?"

Everyone assumed ICE had taken care of me following the ambush. They all looked shocked when I told them I no longer worked for ICE. It was natural to assume law enforcement agencies protect each other and their people. They all were disappointed and in disbelief when I told them what really happened to me. They knew, as I did, that there were hundreds of positions that ICE could have offered me, but didn't. It was obvious they didn't know what to do with me. The Ice Attache office in Mexico had screwed up, and I was a reminder of the mistakes they had made. In truth, they wanted to cover up the entire incident, and I refused to back down. Jaime was dead, and I was living with the aftermath of the shooting every day. I would not let them sweep us under a rug.

Although my own agency seemed to have no use for me, I received a number of prestigious honors for valor and heroism. These included awards for:

- Excellence in Law Enforcement by the ICE Hispanic Agents Association
- Exceptional Performance in Operation Green Horizon
- Meritorious Service Award by the Office of Investigations-El Paso, Texas.
- The Director's Award for Operation in Plain Sight
- Homeland Security Investigations Excellence in Public Service Award
- The ICE Foundation Heroism Award
- The Valor Award by the Federal Law Enforcement Officers Association (FLEOA)
- The Medal of Valor for Outstanding Bravery by the National Latino Peace Officers
- The Medal of Valor by the Hispanic American Police Commanders Officers Association

Of course, I was proud and honored to have all these coveted awards, but it still hurt to be so disrespected and dismissed by the agency I had served for so many years.

I wasn't the only one who was treated this way. One of my friends and colleagues, the one who was the first to come to the hospital after the shooting, wrote "Since the Zapata incident, it seems like those of us who have first-hand knowledge after having stellar careers have now been dismissed or marginalized by ICE." Sad but true.

———

After I retired, calls started coming in for podcast interviews, and I received invitation after invitation to speak at conferences about the shooting.

In 2019, I was contacted to offer commentaries on Fox and other news networks and local television stations. At first, I fielded questions about the shooting, but the broadcasters who talked to me quickly discovered that I have expertise and knowledge beyond that horrifying experience. That's when they started calling on me for commentary about current immigration issues and border security, human trafficking, the caravans that were moving north toward the United States from Central America, the building of the border wall, and other such topics. I enjoyed sharing my expertise and doing my best to help the United States move in the right direction with regard to immigration.

I have also kept in touch with many of the friends and colleagues I made during my years with ICE, and try to keep up with what is going on within the agency.

At one point, ICE directorship changed from James Dinkins to Peter Edge. When the cartel members who had ambushed Jaime and me were about to go on trial in D.C., I sent Peter Edge an invitation by email, asking him to ensure that leadership would attend the trial, as a sign of solidarity. His one-word response was simply, "OK."

But none of the directors—not one high-level official from ICE or DHS — were anywhere to be seen when the trial started. Their obvious lack of support was demoralizing, but not shocking. And yet many Special Agents from all branches of law enforcement were there. So many came, in fact, that they had to open another room to accommodate them all. I felt so supported by the presence of so many of my brothers and sisters in blue.

I recently spoke to Tom Homan, former acting director of ICE, who is now retired, and told him about extending the invitation to Peter Edge and how he had responded. Homan shook his head.

"During the trial, I asked him what was going on with you. He said, 'We can't believe that guy. We've given him everything he's ever wanted, and he's not satisfied. We're through with him.' I didn't really believe him. And I'm so sorry for how you were treated."

There was no reason for Tom to apologize. But I knew that if he had been director at the time, things would have been handled differently.

———

The men who killed Agent Jaime Zapata and severely wounded me were arrested, expedited, and placed on trial in a courtroom in Washington, D.C. It was more than six years after the shooting that the murderers finally faced me in a courtroom, and I was thrilled to think that they were finally going to be brought to justice. It was difficult for me to relive that terrible day, not so much for me, but for Jaime. I wished I had flat-out refused to make that dangerous drive up Highway 57. Yes, most likely that would have been the end of my career. But at least, Jaime would still be alive and, by now, happily married.

The shooters were charged with: Murder, attempted murder and attempted murder of an internationally protected person, as well as weapons charges and aiding and abetting. I don't want to mention their names, because as far as I'm concerned, they don't need to be remembered.

You may recall that after Jaime and I were attacked, the PGR originally claimed that we had been shot in a case of mistaken identity. They said the gunmen had meant to attack the head of the Mexican Federal Police out of San Luis Potosi. I knew this was not the case because our vehicle was armored and bore diplomatic license plates. In addition, I was waving my arms and shouting that we were Americans. and I know they heard me. They didn't care. In fact, after the killing, the shooters were overheard bragging about their belief that they had killed the U.S. ambassador to Mexico.

They had also said that their original plan was to steal the Suburban for the cartel, yet they shot it to pieces with their gun blasts.

Evidence at the trial showed that the murderers were members of a Los Zetas "hit squad" and had been out looking to steal cars on the day of the shooting. According to news reports from the trial, "During the ambush, the cartel members fired at and into the agents' vehicle with handguns and semiautomatic assault weapons, including AK-47 and AR-15 type assault rifles. Investigators later found approximately 90 shell casings at the scene."

I prepared and focused to have the opportunity to testify against them, and by the time the trial was over, it seemed clear to everyone in the courtroom that the defendants were bloodthirsty villains who deserved the harshest possible sentences. Two of the shooters were found guilty of all charges at trial and sentenced to two-consecutive sentences of life in prison. The other shooters group pled guilty and were sentenced to 35, 34, 30, 28 and 12 years behind bars respectively. The Zapata Family and I were out-raged that the shooters didn't get stiffer sentences. We believed they deserved to spend the rest of their lives in prison. But at least they didn't walk free.

At trial, the gunmen admitted that they heard everything I said during the attack. They knew we were Americans — that we were diplomats connected to the U.S. embassy.

Acting Assistant Attorney General Kenneth A. Blanco said, "HSI Special Agents Jaime Zapata and Victor Avila were in Mexico to protect and serve our country when they were ambushed by these ruthless criminals, who will now spend the rest of their lives in a prison cell. This case serves as a reminder, that if you harm a U.S. agent, the U.S. government will pursue you to the ends of the earth to ensure that you are brought to justice."[1]

Attorney Jessie Liu declared, "We have never forgotten what happened to these two American heroes in that ambush on a Mexican highway more than six years ago. The sentencings this

[1] https://www.justice.gov/opa/pr/two-cartel-members-sentenced-life-prison-term -slaying-ice-special-agent-jaime-zapata-and-attempted-muder-of-ice-special-agent-victoravila, accessed July 9, 2020

week reflect our determination to protect U.S. officials abroad and bring to justice those who do them harm."[2]

And Assistant FBI Director Stephen F. Richardson said, "Any attack against a federal agent serving his or her country is deeply personal for us and investigating those attacks remain a top priority for the FBI. I want to thank all of our law enforcement partners and our colleagues at the U.S. Attorney's Office for the District of Columbia for their tireless work to bring this case to a successful conclusion and secure these sentences."[3]

Fine sounding words, of course. But, not so fast. . .

Three years after the trial, all of the defendants appealed their sentences, and, as a result the murder charge was dismissed by the District of Columbia Appellate Court. The court ruled that the murder statute under which they were convicted does not specify whether it applies to acts outside the United States. In May of 2020, just prior to this book's publication, a bill was introduced in Congress to rectify this situation and "clarify the original intent that section 1114 of title 6 18, United States Code, applies extra-territorially. The bill "to further protect officers and employees of the United States," is known as the "Jaime Zapata and Victor Avila Federal Law Enforcement Protection Act." Larry Cosme, President of the Federal Law Enforcement Officers Association (FLEOA) said of the bill, "We are pursuing all avenues to insure justice is served and we appreciate the support of Senator John Cornyn (R-Texas), Representative Henry Cuellar (R-Texas), Representative Peter King (R-New York) and Representative Michael McCaul (R-Texas) to ensure this never happens again."

I'm looking forward to hearing that the murder charges have been reinstated.

———

There were so many shocking developments during our trial. One of the biggest of these was finding out that two of the guns

---

[2] Ibid

[3] Ibid

that were used in the shooting had been trafficked by the ATF, as part of a program called Operation Fast and Furious.

Operation Fast and Furious was developed by the Bureau of Alcohol, Tobacco, Firearms and Explosives. It originated in Phoenix and the idea was to identify and apprehend smugglers running guns from the United States to Mexico. The premise of the program was to allow weapons to walk—make it to Mexico—to find the big fish. In other words, the United States government provided state-of-the-art automatic weapons to cartel members, in hopes that they could track the guns to the criminals, and then arrest them. But there was a problem. The ATF allowed over 2,000 weapons—AK47s, AR15s and, among them, a 50 caliber rifle —to enter Mexico with no follow-through.

You don't let weapons—or drugs—walk.

After I graduated from the academy, one of the first conversations I had with my supervisor—kind of an ICE Agent 101 lesson—included bottom-line advice: If you lose a load of drugs under your watch—drugs we have been following—you will lose your job.

Simple as that.

The same thing goes for weapons. You don't have to be a law enforcement officer to understand it makes no sense to allow weapons to be purchased at gun shops and shows, watch them go into Mexico, and then lose them because no follow-through plan is in place. How are you going to catch the bad guys?

As far as I know, the ATF in Mexico and the Mexican government was never notified. No effort was made to intercept the guns or identify where they were going. Once the shipment crossed the border, it was gone.

These weapons ultimately killed thousands of Mexican citizens and two US agents— Brian Terry, a border patrol agent, and Jaime Zapata. In addition, these weapons turned up at crime scenes around the world, including a mass shooting in Paris, France, in November of 2015, when 137 people were killed and more than 400 were wounded. A 50-caliber rifle from the Fast & Furious shipment was also in El Chapo's possession when the leader of the Sinaloa Drug Cartel was arrested in 2015.

In addition, many American gun shops that cooperated with the ATF were ruined. They were told to sell guns to the suspicious characters, and then prosecuted for doing so. When the government was through with them, they were discarded by the government and left to face the consequences. In some instances, the ATF took their documents and never pursued any investigation. Operation Fast and Furious is the prime example of our own government circumventing the very law they enforce.

As you can see, Operation Fast & Furious was an astounding failure.

––––––

Whenever a Special Agent is involved in an incident of any kind, ICE opens an internal investigation. For example, if an agent has an accident in an agency vehicle, there is an investigation. Even if the local police are involved, ICE still conducts its own separate investigation. If an agent drives while under the influence, ICE does an investigation.

So, where were they? An agent had been killed in the line of duty and another had been critically wounded ... and ICE hadn't done anything.

A colleague of mine was unrelenting in his pressure to get ICE Mexico City to open an investigation—and finally succeeded. Multiple interviews were conducted with the ICE personnel in Mexico and with anyone who had even a peripheral involvement, but no one interviewed me. How was that possible? I was the only eye-witness, the only person who knew what had happened, and no one interviewed me.

At one point, while I was in the hospital, the FBI had interviewed me for purposes of their criminal investigation. Standard operating procedure is to conduct follow-up interviews, but I never heard anything further.

A couple of years ago, I was so exasperated I contacted the Office of Special Counsel (OSC) in Washington, DC. I submitted my allegations and concerns and requested an internal investigation into wrongdoing by ICE management in the incident. OSC agreed that an investigation should be opened and referred the matter to ICE.

The OSC inquiry prompted ICE/HIS to investigate my allegations. Internal Affairs interviewed me, and three of my six allegations were substantiated. This was huge progress. Prior to this I had told my story over and over, and no one would corroborate anything I said.

There had been gross mismanagement in our office, and Jaime and I had paid a terrible price. Yet somehow, even with one agent lost and another critically injured, that case made my supervisors' careers. They are both now Special Agents in Charge. The deputy Attaché currently runs the Miami office, and the Attaché heads the office in New Orleans. In my opinion, their promotions prove the adage, "Screw up in the government and you get promoted."

What hurt most was that when the OSC finally released the interviews from 2011 — the interviews I hadn't been privy to — I was sickened by the audacity of the lies.

The Attaché stated to internal affairs that he had instructed me regarding which route to follow – which was false – and the deputy Attaché denied knowing about the security issues with Highway 57. That, too, was patently false. And my immediate supervisor, Simon, said he had volunteered to go to Monterrey in my place, and I refused the offer. *What?!* No one *volunteered* for the assignment. If he — or anyone — had offered to go, I would have immediately — and gladly — accepted. I never wanted to go on the trip. I didn't want *anyone* to go.

Their statements were in direct opposition to an alert sent to all U.S. personnel by the U.S. Ambassador via the Regional Security Officer on January 18, 2011, in which he stated:

- Travel by vehicle from the U.S. border to interior Posts (Monterrey, Mazatlán, Merida, Mexico City and Guadalajara) is prohibited. There is no acceptable alternate route. The opposite also applies, personnel and family members from these interior Posts cannot travel to the U.S. Border.
- Official travel by personnel already assigned to Post to prohibited travel areas must be coordinated with the

appropriate RSO and conform to Mission policy. Note: Official travel cannot be used as a loophole to transport employee or family members (in a POV or armored GOV) to/from an interior Post as it relates to the U.S. Border.

So much for not being aware that there was any danger.

Contrary to testimony given by my superiors, I received no briefing on the assignment other than to pick up the equipment in Monterrey and return it to Mexico City on the same day. Briefing is one of the most important aspects of any assignment. Intricate details regarding an operational plan, as well as the specific part each agent will play, are paramount components of a briefing. If an agent doesn't attend a briefing, he or she will not be included in the operation.

"If you're not present for the briefing, you don't get to play" is something we often say. Miss the briefing and you're not allowed to play police and knock down doors. Unfortunate and deadly occurrences have resulted—including agents being shot by friendly fire—when someone wasn't briefed on everyone's role in the plan.

That all-important briefing never happened for me or for Jaime. We had no operational plan—no backup—none of the precautions that would have been taken on any other day. My supervisors wanted that equipment quickly because they had something going on with the Operation Pacific Rim case. They were clouded by the glory of what a successful outcome could mean for their careers. And Jaime and I paid the price for their ambition.

Part Two

A PLAN TO STRENGTHEN
OUR BORDER SECURITY

Chapter Ten

FOREIGN TERRORIST ORGANIZATIONS

I have heard from and talked to many people who think that anyone who is opposed to illegal immigration is racist. They seem to think that America should simply open her borders and welcome anyone who wants to come here. That might be the case if we lived in a perfect world. But our world is far from perfect.

Our current immigration policies are harmful in so many ways. They cause harm to our country and our people, and they hurt the people from Mexico — and other countries — who try to sneak across our borders to build a better life for themselves and their families. Our policies are harmful because some of those who come across our borders are not looking for a better life at all, but are criminals and drug dealers who will endanger American families and communities. More than 70,000 Americans die from drug overdoses every year. Do we really want to increase the death toll?

Some of those who want to come into this country are bloodthirsty killers who have turned life in Mexico and Central America into a living hell for millions of their fellow countrymen. I've already described some of what I encountered during my time in Mexico. Headless bodies hanging from highway overpasses. Mass graves filled with rotting corpses. Dozens of murders every day in cities like Ciudad Juarez. Do we really want to see this kind of terror taking place in the United States?

Our current policies are also dangerous for the illegal aliens themselves, many of whom die in their attempts to reach the United

States. Hundreds have perished trying to cross the deserts into the southwestern United States. Who knows how many have died after being abandoned by coyotes, who left them crowded into truck trailers, without food, water, or any escape from the heat?

And finally, our policies are dangerous for Mexican children, who are used as bargaining chips by illegals who claim to be their parents, but aren't really. And for young girls who are trafficked into the United States and coerced into sexual slavery.

In other words, our current policies are a mess – and immediate steps are necessary to fix them. Over the next section of this book, I plan to give some practical steps for shoring up our borders and making life better for innocent, law-abiding citizens, both in Mexico and here in the United States.

Some people will tell you that the first thing we have to do is build a strong, impenetrable wall along the border between the United States and Mexico. I agree that the wall is important – and must be completed soon. (More about that in the next chapter.) But there is something else that can and should be done immediately. The United States must designate some Mexican cartels as foreign terrorist organizations.

Consider that in 2018, the Taliban controlled an estimated 46 percent of Afghanistan, and thousands of American troops were stationed there to fight them. But in the same year, the Mexican government admitted that 80 percent of its territory was controlled, or partly controlled, by the various drug cartels.[4] In fact, according to some experts, all of the major smuggling areas leading into California, Arizona, New Mexico and Texas are controlled by the cartels. And there are other similarities between the cartels and organizations that have officially been labeled as terrorist organizations by the United States. For example, the Zetas cartel alone has killed more people than Al Qaeda or ISIS ever did. And although ISIS was known for its barbaric brutality, its leaders have absolutely nothing on the vicious drug kings of Mexico. They systematically terrorize through rape, extortion, kidnapping and

---

[4] https://www.conservativereview.com/news/mexican-government-admits-80-populated-territory-run-cartels-including-key-border-areas/accessed July 9, 2020

murder. They use gruesome tactics — like displaying the body parts of their victims in public places — to control the local citizenry. They have firefights in broad daylight without any regard for innocent citizens.

The only difference between ISIS and the Mexican cartels, as far as I can see, is that Islamic State's ideology is religion, and the cartels' ideology is drugs, money and power. Mostly money.

Now, some people have suggested that if we labeled the cartels as terrorist organizations, it follows that we would then send American troops into Mexico to fight them. This is not the case. What the terrorist designation means is that organizations actively combating cartels would receive finances and resources to help them. It would also allow agencies to seize cartels' key assets and funds. And who knows? If we back away and let the cartels continue to grow unchecked, we may soon reach the point where we have to send troops into Mexico!

It might surprise you to know that Mexico's drug cartels launder billions of dollars of "dirty money" through major banks in the United States and Europe each year. Much of this "ill-gotten gain" passes through the system with no questions asked. In 2012, HSBC Bank was fined for laundering $881 million of dirty money from these cartels.[5]

You see, after the cartels sell their drugs in the United States or other countries, they need a way to get the money back into Mexico — and they must do it secretly. One of the ways they do this is by sending their drug proceeds to financial institutions through wire transfers made in a variety of different names. At the same time, they vary the size of their deposits to make it harder for authorities to follow the paper trail. They also do this because any deposit over $10,000 must be reported to the Internal Revenue Service.

Do you believe that American and international banks are unwittingly helping the cartels?

If so, I have some swamp land in Florida to sell you!

---

[5] https://www.reuters.com/article/us-hsbc-usa/hsbc-draws-line-under-mexican-cartel-case-after-five-years-on-probation, accessed July 9, 2020

Another way they get cash back into Mexico is to smuggle it across the border. Sometimes they fill trucks with money and send them south. Once time in El Paso, a truck was stopped with $5 million in cash. Drugs and illegals are headed north, and money goes south.

The cartels are raking in billions of dollars every year, and it is very hard for some banks – or bankers – to resist that kind of money. I do not believe that financial institutions are cooperating with the cartels out of ignorance. It is obviously deliberate. If we were to freeze—and seize—all the illicit funds attributed to the cartels, numerous businesses would go bankrupt. Banks on the American side of the border in El Paso and McAllen, Texas, for example would experience recession.

Plus, if the cartels are designated as terrorist groups, as President Trump has said he plans to do, it would then be illegal for any American to intentionally provide support. Financial institutions would be barred from doing any type of business with a cartel or any of its members, and those who broke the law would face long prison sentences.

Derek Maltz, former Special Agent in charge of the Drug Enforcement Administration Special Operations Division in New York, told Fox News, "The Foreign Terrorist Organization designation is an important step in a positive direction for US national security. Too many Americans have died as the ruthless cartels have made billions by terrorizing communities and killing at unprecedented levels. It's clear President Trump always places the safety of Americans first. Designating the cartels as terrorists and implementing a focused operational plan will save a tremendous amount of lives."[6]

Fox News also pointed out that the Foreign Terrorist Organization tag "could also mean that an American in an inner-city gang selling street drugs that originated from south of the border could be prosecuted under anti-terrorism laws – possibly

---

[6] https://www.foxnews.com/world/mexican-cartels-foreign-terrorist-organization-impact, accessed July 9, 2020

being given a life sentence." Wouldn't it be great to get gangsters off the streets and into jail where they belong?

Calling and designating cartels as what they are—terrorists— would allow the United States government to enforce their eradication very differently than they are currently able to do. Right now, it is illegal to associate or have any form of relationship with a terrorist or terrorist organization, so if a citizen communicates with ISIS, the FBI will be all over him. I believe it should be the same for anyone who communicates with one of the drug cartels. That way, if someone is dealing drugs in St. Louis, and those drugs can be connected to a cartel, the dealer could be convicted of associating with a terrorist organization. He would be considered part of the cartel and prosecuted under that statute. This means he or she would face a much stiffer sentence than the law currently allows.

Instead of facing a sentence of two or three years for pushing drugs, guilty parties would be sent to prison for decades or even life. This would have a major effect on dealers in America, reducing both the violence and the influx of drugs, as the majority of drug dealers and illegal drug-related organizations are clearly linked to a cartel in some way. While some are directly associated, there are gangs who work independently yet are still connected to a cartel simply because of the product they sell.

For example, say a drug dealer is picked up by the local police and an investigation reveals that the dealer is connected to a gang pushing a particular drug. That drug can be traced to a certain cartel. Now that drug dealer—and the gang—is considered part of the cartel. The dealer might protest that he was only selling dime bags of cocaine or a couple of bags of methamphetamines. But once it was determined that those drugs came from the Sinaloa cartel, the dealer would be considered to be a member of that cartel. Once we begin picking up the dealers and gang members, they will not want to be allied with a terrorist cartel, especially once they know they can be put in jail for life for that association.

This plan would require massive coordination on the part of all federal, state, and local law enforcement agencies and would be a cumbersome task. Yet, the outcome would change the face of cartel criminal activity in our country.

Use of force would be a last resort but could be employed in the event the cartels fight back. Without setting boots on the ground, the United States could use drones to destroy meth labs and cocaine fields.

The FTO designation would result in creating a major dent in cartel activity in the US. While we might not succeed in shutting them all down, it would inflict significant damage and go a long way to reduce the amount of drugs coming into our country.

———

Shutting down and dismantling drug cartels operating in the United States is a multi-faceted and complex issue. In the past fifteen to twenty years, cartels have changed their strategies and movements. Major players in the trafficking of heroin, cocaine, marijuana, fentanyl, and methamphetamines, have expanded their criminal activities to include human trafficking, money laundering, and, surprisingly, even the avocado trade.

Mexico is of no help in curbing cartel activity spawned in-country. As I mentioned earlier, 80 percent of Mexico is influenced and controlled by the cartels, especially in the urban areas. A few years ago, the Mexican government declared war on the cartels, challenging them to some extent, but was totally ineffective in taking them out.

The current president of Mexico, Andreas Manuel Lopez-Obrador, (they call him AMLO) has basically admitted he plans to do nothing about the cartels. He'd rather give them hugs than bullets and feels they are not to be defied. The government administration has become a servant to the cartels and is complicit in the drug trade. In effect, the president himself works for them.

Meanwhile, I have just read that the criminals of the Sinaloa Cartel and the Cartel Jalisco Nueva Genaración (CJNG), probably the most dangerous cartel in the world, are trying to win over the people by handing out care packages full of food, soap and other basic supplies. The bags apparently have a photo of their former leader, the murderous El Chapo, on one side and the initials of the cartel on the other. They want ordinary people to think of them as angels, when, in reality, they are devils who don't mind killing innocent civilians in the most brutal and horrendous ways. I have seen a video in which they executed one of their rivals by setting him on fire. They have absolutely no compassion, and we can't just walk away and let them wage a public relations war for the hearts and minds of the Mexican people.

With virtually no law enforcement, there has been a dramatic change in who is prosecuted in Mexico and who isn't. When a crime is committed in the United States, the incident is investigated, evidence is collected, an arrest is made, and someone is prosecuted. Not so in Mexico. Police may respond to the scene, collect evidence, and perhaps pick up suspects, but—in ninety-eight percent of the cases—no one is prosecuted. Murder. Rape. Theft. Victims of vicious crimes have only a two-percent likelihood of seeing justice. And cartels continue their reign of terror without fear of repercussions.

Taking a page from the playbook of Colombia's Pablo Escobar, cartels ingratiate themselves to some citizens of Mexico through relief efforts and becoming part of their daily way of life. Yet they maintain tight control through fear and coercion. Homicides are through the roof with thousands of blameless people killed and over 65,000 missing in 2019 alone. Savage methods include public hangings, acid baths, and beheading. While these deaths are often reported as cartel-on-cartel or cartel-versus-police violence, the majority of—let's call them what they are—*murders* are perpetrated on innocent citizens for the sole purpose of intimidation. Cartels have been known to hang signs on their victims labeling them as rival cartel members and even dress the dead in police uniforms and pronounce them to be corrupt officers.

Cartels do not hesitate to take advantage of social media. For example, they are adept at using You Tube to get their message out. They show images of atrocities and threats to instill terror in the hearts of the populace. Recruitment focuses heavily on ex-military officers with offers of better pay, benefits, and the promise that, in the event of the recruit's death, families will be well cared for. All in all, a much better deal than what the government provides.

For many years, Mexico was a transit country—drugs were manufactured and then smuggled to other countries. But the status quo has deteriorated in the last ten to fifteen years. Drug abuse statistics have skyrocketed, as Mexicans have become users as well. Add widespread addiction to the proliferation of dealers, corruption, persistent economic crisis, and the crime rate rises even further.

At one point, it was hoped that the legalization of marijuana in some American states would have a significant impact in curbing illegal drug traffic. Not so. Legalization has increased demand, thereby increasing supply, and revenues are through the roof. Unfortunately, with more people taking advantage of relaxed laws, DUIs have also skyrocketed. Today's marijuana is not the marijuana of the 60s but is much more powerful and a lot more addictive.

It used to be that criminal investigators intent on dismantling the cartels would open cases, then build investigations over the course of a year or two with the goal of identifying the higher players in an organization. These long-term investigations made little difference and are no longer substantiated. We must find another way.

Chapter Eleven

BUILD THE WALL

One of President Trump's most important campaign promises in 2016 was to build a wall along the border between the United States and Mexico. I believe that it was this pledge, more than anything else that propelled him into the White House.

Many people have fought against the building of the wall since Trump first brought up the subject but that does not change the fact that this is a good idea. Building a wall is not, as some claim, a racist act. It is not anti-Mexico or anti-Hispanic. It is a practical way to protect the United States from the criminals who want to infest our country and create the same kind of destruction and havoc they have wreaked in their home country. Plus, the wall will not be built to keep Mexicans out of our country. Illegals from countries around the world are coming into the United States through our Southern border, and our desire is to stop all of these people who, for some reason, refuse to go through legal channels to get here.

Some people make the point that the United States owes a great deal to its immigrant population, and they won't get an argument from me. However, the immigrants who helped make this country great have come into the United States through legal channels. They filled out the proper forms and waited until their turn came. That's one of the reasons why you will find so many Mexican-Americans who are opposed to illegal immigration. They came into the United States in an orderly, proper way, but they look around and see thousands upon thousands of people trying to cut in line. Imagine if you were standing in line at a drinking fountain, so thirsty you felt like you were about to faint, but other people were crowding in front of you. Would you be happy for them? Would you cheer when you saw them drinking that clear, cool water, while your throat remained parched and dry? I don't think so. I have a feeling that you would be yelling at them, "Hey! Quit cutting in line!"

The United States is not trying to close its borders to all immigrants. Legal immigration is a good thing. Those of us who favor the building of a wall just want immigrants to obey our laws, and apply to come into this country legally – which is exactly what my parents did.

As you may recall, when President Trump was campaigning for office, he said of illegal aliens: "They're bringing drugs. They're bringing crime. They're rapists. And some, I assume, are good people." [7] He spoke plainly and forcefully – some said he was too plain and too forceful – but he told the truth. Some illegals are bringing drugs and crime into America. Not all are rapists, robbers and murderers. I saw much proof of this during my years with ICE. President Trump was not being a demagogue. He was telling the truth, and the American people responded because they knew it.

Since then, the wall has become a divisive political statement. Democrats have labeled it as a symbol of anti-immigration, condemning it as an immoral act. Republicans herald it as a symbol of America's greatness, touting its ability to end the drug war.

Unfortunately, these viewpoints are not accurate. The wall is being built and it will *help* stem the tide of crime and drugs that flow into the United States every day. And yet, a wall is only part of a much larger solution, a solution that includes dismantling cartels, ending sanctuary cities, and stopping the practice of catch and release for illegal immigrants.

A border wall will not completely end illegal immigration into the United States, but it is a necessary tool (similar to drones and sensors) that would help agents protect our border. Right now,

---

[7] https://www.foxnews.com/world/mexican-cartels-foreign-terrorist-organization-impact, accessed July 9, 2020

border patrol agents have too much ground to cover and too few resources. Hundreds of miles of border are unpatrolled every day. Essentially, a wall would act as a funnel, forcing smugglers to certain areas in their attempts to cross the border. American agents could then focus their resources and efforts on those areas, making it easier to apprehend and detain criminals.

Now, there are places along the Mexican border where there are fences and other barriers to keep people from coming into the United States illegally. Some of these work quite well. But the problem is that there are other places where there are no barriers at all, and anyone who wants to cross can do so easily. The entire border is over 1,900 miles long, and we've tried to fix our problem with illegal immigration by slapping a few Band-Aids here and there. For our own safety and protection, we need one unified wall along the entire length of the border, and that's what I like most about the wall that Donald Trump is building.

You can take it from me, there are some very dangerous people in Mexico. It is naïve to think that all those who are coming into our country illegally are just hard-working men and women who want to build a better life for their families. Many are, yes. But others are violent criminals who have destroyed much of their own country, and now they want to do the same thing here. We can't let that happen!

Now, I doubt if there is anyone who believes that a wall will completely stop the flow of illegal immigrants into the United States. But it will certainly slow the traffic down and give Border Patrol agents time to respond. The way it is right now, much of our southern border is completely porous. There is nothing at all to mark its presence. Not even a flimsy barbed wire fence. Sure, people can probably find a way to get over a 20-foot wall — but it won't be easy and it will take time.

I have seen huge trucks full of drugs go crashing across the border without even slowing down. That couldn't happen if a sturdy wall were in place.

A wall would also prevent the type of thing that happens where people who have crossed the border illegally are apprehended, released into Mexico, and then immediately come back into the United States. I have seen cases where the same person was arrested for crossing the border illegally two or three times in one day. That's how easy it is to get across the border in some parts of the Southwest. It certainly wouldn't be that way if we had a 20-foot tall wall along the border. (By the way, I am convinced that we must also stop our "catch and release" policies that allow illegals to come back into the country again and again. More about that later.)

In his book, *Defend the Border and Save Lives*,[8] my friend Tom Homan, Former Director of ICE, writes, "Without a wall, our border is a revolving door for bad guys. Gang members and those with criminal records don't usually drive through legal ports of entry, because they know our database continues to improve. One particular arrest from my career comes to mind. The man was missing several fingers on his right hand. He told me he'd lost them in a farming accident. I arrested him around nine o'clock in the morning on the east side of the port of entry, processed him — an experienced agent could process an illegal alien in just twenty minutes — and drove him back to the border. A couple hours later, I arrested him coming over the west side of the port of entry. We processed him again. We sent him back. That afternoon, a sensor went off in an area outside my patrol, but the other agent was busy. As I drove up to the man, he turned to me and started laughing. By now, we had a pretty good routine, and I processed him in record time.

"Later that afternoon, an agent walked into the office with an arrestee. "Did you just arrest him?" I asked. "Yeah, do you know this guy?" "You could say that. I arrested him three times today." On the surface, this might sound like a funny story. The problem is, this happens every day on sections of our border that do not have a wall. When you hear yet another horrible news report about violence committed by an illegal alien who was "previously deported six times," think about the need for a border wall.

During the Clinton Administration, a wall was built along the border between San Diego and Tijuana. This was a place where

---

[8] Homan, Tom, "Defend the Border and Save Lives," (Center Street) 2020

hundreds of illegals poured into the United States every day – far too many to be stopped. Our Border Patrol agents were completely outmanned and overwhelmed.

A tall fence made of steel was erected along the border, and illegals are no longer swarming into the United States there. This is proof that walls work. And according to BorderFacts.com, in four areas where physical barriers along the border have been expanded – El Paso, Yuma, Tucson and San Diego — illegal traffic has dropped by at least 90 percent.

Now you may have done a double-take when I said the fence in San Diego was built during the Clinton administration. Was that a misprint? No! The fact is that Bill Clinton considered himself to be strong on border security. So did Barack Obama, who bragged that his administration had strengthened border security "beyond what many thought was possible." He also said, "We now have more boots on the ground on the southwest border than at any time in our history."[9] And Hillary Clinton said, "I voted many times when I was a senator to spend money to build a barrier to try to prevent illegal aliens from coming in."[10]

It seems that there was once a time when almost everyone seemed to agree that a wall along our southern border was a good idea. What happened? The pendulum has been pushed far to the left. I think it's important to find out who has done the pushing and why. All I know is that the cartels are certainly not in favor of a wall.

———

One of the common objections to the border wall, one I hear often, is that it is way too expensive – that the money should be used for positive things – like education and fighting hunger. I don't know anyone who would be against providing the best

[9] https://www.nationalreview.com/corner/scathing-denunciation-of-obama-administrations-immigration-enforcement/ accessed July 9, 2020.

[10] https://www.washingtonexaminer.com/weekly-standard/hillary-i-voted-for-border-fence-to-keep-out-illegal-immigrants, accessed July 9, 2020.

possible educational system for our children, and I think it's a disgrace that there are families in this, the greatest country in the world, that don't have enough to eat. But I think it's disingenuous to blame the wall for these ills, or to say that if we didn't build the wall we could feed every hungry American.

Education is important, fighting hunger and poverty is important, but so is tightening our borders to keep out dangerous criminals and drug dealers.

And besides, the $10 billion it costs to build the wall could be easily repaid within ten years of its completion. Currently, ICE spends roughly $2 billion per year on detention. Existence of a border wall would greatly reduce that cost, perhaps by as much as one-half. In other words, if we saved $1 billion per year on detention – a figure that seems reasonable – the wall would be paid for in ten years. And, according to the American Federation for Immigration Reform, the current cost of illegal immigration to the United States is $116 billion per year.

Imagine if we could remove those costs from our annual expenses.

In my opinion, building a border wall is far less expensive than living without one.

The absence of a wall along our southern border creates so many problems. For example, I have responded to numerous cases involving what we call "drive-thrus." This is where large SUVs are loaded to maximum capacity with drugs, driven directly across the border – without opposition — and unloaded. Someone else then picks up the drugs and moves them further into the United States. The drug dealers can do this because it is physically impossible for our agents to do what a wall could do – which is be present at every mile of the border to stop the bad guys. Furthermore, an old-fashioned fence can't withstand the force generated by an SUV that weighs more than 6,000 pounds, but a wall that's 20-feet tall could.

I've also seen teenage boys carrying drugs into the United States in backpacks. They simply walk across the border, drop the drugs off in the brush for their American counterparts to pick up, and then they walk back into Mexico.

The fact is that right now, it is much too easy to get across the border, and there are rattlesnakes on the other side that must be kept out of this country. I know that anyone who had seen a fraction of the brutality and violence I've seen in Mexico would be totally in favor of building a wall.

Now, let me tell you that I am a people person and always have been. I like being around other people. Over the last few weeks as I've been writing this book, most of the United States has been sheltering in place due to the COVID-19 pandemic. Even though I love being at home with Claudia and the children, this has been a difficult time for me, because I enjoy hanging out with my friends. I'm telling you this because I want you to know that my desire to see a wall built across our southern border has nothing to do with my feelings about people in general. I would love to trust everyone and think the best about everyone – but my experience shows me that I can't. Nor can I believe everything they tell me. Doing that could bring danger to other people I care about and love.

Many people who try to come into the United States say they can't be sent back to Mexico (or wherever else they come from) because their lives would be in danger. For the most part, that's not true. Refugees from Latin America come here because they want to better themselves economically – and you can't really blame them for that, because many of them live in abject poverty. But it is not true that if we return them to their home countries we are sending them to a certain death — and we can't let our compassion get the best of us and cause us to make decisions that are detrimental to our country. Yes, there are countries where this may be true. Syria, for example, and other countries in the Middle East. I believe we should give first consideration to those who are going to face persecution, and perhaps even death, if they are sent back home – but, again, this is not true of those who come here from Latin America. A border wall will save lives – not take them.

———

Before we move on to talk about sanctuary cities, I want to say a brief word about something that has become a very emotional issue for many people – and that is the separation of families that supposedly takes place at border crossings. I'm not sure that this issue has much to do with the building of a wall – but this is as good a place as any to talk about it.

Did you know that when ICE and the Border Patrol teamed up to do some DNA testing at the border, they found that many of the "families" waiting for entrance into the United States were not really related. That's right. They were fakes! My friend Tom Homan says, "When I was the director at ICE, we had plenty of cases just like this where cartels and family members would rent children to single adults so they could cross illegally and be released. Incredible, and unthinkable, but very true."[11] In fact, some of these children were rented out several times! Other studies showed that nearly a third of the families coming to our border were not families at all, and that many supporting documents were counterfeit.

One time, when I was still working in El Paso, we got a tip that a local motel was being used to stash undocumented aliens who were waiting for transportation deeper into the United States. Sure enough, there were at least 15 adults waiting in that motel. We arrested the smuggler without incident and took the illegals back to the station to process them into the system.

As we were doing this, one of the women started yelling in Spanish, "He has my child! Help me find my daughter!"

When I asked her what she was talking about, she told me with tears in her eyes that she had let the smuggler borrow her 18-month-old daughter to help someone get across the border into the United States. Now she was terrified that she would never see her child again. We put some pressure on the guy, who finally admitted that the woman was telling the truth – and gave us an address where we could find the child.

---

[11] Homan, "Defend the Border and Save Lives."

We quickly donned our gear and headed out to the house in question. We had no idea what kind of resistance we were going to find when we got there.

The address belonged to a small, nondescript house in an ordinary neighborhood. The lawn was neat and tidy. A path of stones led across the lawn to the front door. My team and I quietly approached the front door.

We held our breath and listened. It sounded like a daycare center in there! Children were laughing, crying, screaming. There must have been dozens of kids in there.

With our guns at the ready, we pushed the door open and hurried inside.

The place was full of kids, just as it sounded. Not dozens, perhaps, but at least 15 or 20 of them, from babies on up to boys and girls of six or seven years old. They didn't even seem to notice us.

My partner and I made our way through the house, looking for the smugglers involved. We knocked on every closed door and then opened it, shouting, "Police! Police! At the end of the hall, a bedroom door was slightly open, so I pushed it open further and entered.

Someone moved in the dark. Was someone waiting to ambush me in there? I tightened my grip on my gun. I flipped on the light with my other hand and saw that a middle-aged blonde woman was lying on the bed with a tiny girl who turned out to be the daughter of the woman who had sent us here. "I almost killed you!" I shouted. "You scared me!"

We found out that the blonde woman worked for the smugglers. Her job was to find children who could help would-be immigrants get across the U.S. border. It still makes me cringe when I think about how close I came to shooting her. Such is the reality of life along the U.S.-Mexican border.

In many cases we are not separating families, but rather, rescuing children from adults who are trafficking them or otherwise using them for their own gain.

You may remember seeing, a few months ago, a photograph in the newspaper of a young girl and her father floating face down in the Rio Grande River. These were two immigrants from

Mexico who were trying to get across the river and didn't make it. After the photograph appeared in newspapers across the United States, there was an outcry against ICE. Somehow, the agency was blamed for causing this tragedy. But the truth is that our Border Patrol agents do everything they can to prevent these kinds of tragedies. Just about every day, our agents pull drowned bodies from rivers like the Rio Grande, and many of them are children.

El Paso is an especially dangerous place to cross the border because the Rio Grande is very tricky. Even on days when it doesn't look like there's much water in the river, the current can pull you down. And then, once you get across the river, you have to contend with the deep, swift-flowing Franklin Canal. It can be too much, especially if you're exhausted from fighting your way across the Rio Grande. The men and women of our border patrol are rescuing people every day – but, tragically, they can't rescue everyone who needs their help.

As a father myself, it breaks my heart to think of any child dying in this way. But if there is any blame, I think it belongs to the parents who put their children in such danger and not to the men and women who are putting themselves on the line to guard our borders. Besides, I've seen members of our Border Patrol go out of their way to keep families and their children safe. They provide blankets for the kids, diapers for families with babies, sanitary supplies for women – they spend so much of their time helping people in need, but then they are vilified and treated like monsters. It's not fair.

Chapter Twelve

STOP SANCTUARY CITIES

S anctuary sounds like a noble idea – almost holy. It's a place where innocent creatures can find refuge from those who seek to destroy them. We're all familiar with wildlife sanctuaries where rare animals are protected from hunters. The center of every church is the sanctuary , where worshipers come together into the restorative presence of God. A sanctuary is a safe place where, for a time, we can escape the trials and tribulations that life brings to us all.

And so, when we first hear the term, "sanctuary cities," it sounds like a good thing.

But it's not.

In the United States, sanctuary cities are places where criminals are protected from the law. Where people who are in the United States illegally are sheltered and kept from being sent back to their countries of origin, even though that would be far better for the United States and, in many instances, the refugees themselves. Some people seem to think that our sanctuary cities are full of frail Mexican women and children – gentle people who just need an opportunity to start over in life. And some illegal aliens in this country fit that description. But there are also thousands of criminals – robbers, burglars, thieves and other dangerous people who are protected by elected officials and individuals who are making a terrible mistake.

Sanctuary cities, by definition, are supposed to provide protection, support, and asylum to refugees. Unfortunately, in the United States, they have evolved into something else entirely.

Instead of protecting refugees, they protect criminals, and because they do, the policies of sanctuary cities often have the opposite of their intended effect. Essentially, when illegal immigrants are detained or interdicted, they are often released, *whether or not they have a criminal record*. Hardened criminals know about these policies, and they take advantage of them.

There are many things about sanctuary cities that I find disturbing and distasteful. One of these is that they are built on the premise that the men and women of ICE are enemies of decent, law-abiding people. This is not at all true. Nor is ICE a racist organization. We do not suspect that every person with dark skin is an undocumented alien or a criminal. And, even though a majority of America's recent undocumented immigrants come from South of the Border, we also know that we have plenty of illegals in the United States who came into this country from Europe, the Middle East, Russia and other countries around the world. Our goal is to make America's cities safer for all law-abiding citizens, no matter where they were born or what language they speak.

Some liberals will tell you that sanctuary cities are safer than non-sanctuary cities because many Hispanics and people of other ethnicities who live in those cities are afraid of the police. If a crime is committed against them, they say, they won't report it because they fear that the police will turn on them and they will be deported. In a sanctuary city they feel much more at ease about talking to the police and so crime rates are lower. Really? Try telling that to Kate Steinle's family. In all my years as an ICE agent, I never saw an instance of what I would call police brutality. Yes, I had some issues with some of the people I worked with. But, never because they were mean or racist. My feeling is that if an immigrant in an American city is afraid to call the police, it must be because of what he or she experienced at the hands of the police in his or her own country. Sanctuary cities are not an antidote to fear of the police. The best way to help people trust the police would be some good old-fashioned community service work to demonstrate the truth of what every first-grader knows: "The policeman is your friend."

———

The biggest objection I have to sanctuary cities is that their policies leave ordinary, law-abiding citizens in danger. We have enough crime in the United States without bringing in criminals from all over the world and giving them a safe place from which to carry out their criminal activities.

There is a myth that ICE agents are engaging in massive crackdowns, where they are sweeping into cities and rounding up every illegal and either putting them in jail or sending them to their country of origin. This is simply not true. Many local and state officials have ordered their police departments not to cooperate with ICE. ICE Agents have been labeled as the bad guys of the immigration debate and are often reviled by those they are trying to protect. Consider this: It is "common knowledge" that there have been far more deportations during the Trump Administration than under Barack Obama. But this "common knowledge" is not true. The truth is that there were far more deportations under Obama – approximately 3 million of them — but the left's media machine has convinced many otherwise.

ICE is not a threat to the immigrant population. In fact, we are looking for illegal criminal aliens who prey on law-abiding citizens and also commit crimes against their own immigrant communities. They make life in sanctuary cities miserable for the immigrants who live there.

When I was an ICE-HSI Special Agent, I never arrested anyone solely for being in the country illegally. Everyone I arrested had committed a crime. I arrested plenty of people on other charges who were also in this country illegally. But I took them into custody because they were dealing drugs, smuggling humans, trafficking humans, money laundering, etc.

In cities that have not proclaimed themselves as sanctuary cities, ICE is notified the moment an illegal alien is arrested, and therefore is able to lodge a detainer. This detainer then allows ICE agents to interview, detain and/or swiftly remove that person from the country once he has fulfilled his sentence. However, sanctuary cities refuse to notify and cooperate with ICE, and this policy has horrifying consequences. Many of these criminals go on to rape or murder innocent American citizens. In other words, instead of protecting innocents, sanctuary cities often lead to the exploitation and destruction of innocent American citizens. The ineffective and immoral policies need to stop.

In sanctuary cities like Los Angeles, Chicago, Baltimore and Houston, when an illegal immigrant is arrested on a charge—theft, rape, selling drugs, murder, DUI, family violence, assault, whatever it may be – he or she is processed through the criminal system like an American citizen. In other words, they are arrested by local police, processed, and then released on bail with a set court date. Of course, most of these illegals then skip town and are never seen again, unless they are arrested for another criminal offense somewhere down the line – as many are.

Consider the tragic case of Kate Steinle, a young woman who was shot and killed on July 1, 2015, as she walked with her father and a family friend along Pier 14 in the Embarcadero District of San Francisco. Kate, just 32 years of age, died at San Francisco General Hospital after being shot by an illegal alien named Jose Inez Garcia-Zarate. The killer claimed the shooting was an accident that occurred when the gun he was holding discharged accidentally. The bullet struck Ms. Steinle in the back, severing an aorta. She fell to the pavement, screaming for her father, who performed CPR on her before an ambulance arrived. She died two hours later. She was a bright, beautiful young woman with a good job and a promising future ahead of her, but her life was foolishly cut short.

Garcia-Zarate claimed that he had found the gun, just moments before the shooting, wrapped in a T-shirt beneath the bench he was sitting on. He said it went off as he was picking it up. The shooter, who was arrested and charged with first degree murder, was a convicted felon, who admitted that he was in a stupor after taking sleeping pills he found in a dumpster. A subsequent investigation revealed that he had been deported five times after entering the

United States illegally. In addition, he had seven felony convictions, mostly for drug violations such as felony heroin possession and manufacturing narcotics. He was on probation in Texas at the time of the shooting. He was one of those guys who just couldn't stay out of trouble – and it seems he couldn't stay out of the United States either.

On March 26, 2015, just four months before the shooting, Garcia-Zarate had been turned over to San Francisco authorities to finish out a jail sentence for an outstanding drug warrant. At that time, ICE entered a detainer for him, asking that he be kept in custody until immigration authorities could pick him up. But because San Francisco is a sanctuary city, authorities would not cooperate with ICE, and the agency was not notified when Garcia-Zarate was released from San Francisco County Jail on April 15, 2015. In other words, if San Francisco had not been a sanctuary city, ICE would have dealt with the man and Kate Steinle would be alive and well today.

At his trial, the killer first claimed that he had been shooting at sea lions, which are a favorite tourist attraction at Pier 14. Because California sea lions are a protected species, he could have been jailed for up to a year and fined $25,000 for that offense. He then changed his story to claim that he had found the gun under a bench, and that it had gone off as he was picking it up.

What happened next? Garcia-Zarate was found not guilty of murder or the lesser charge of manslaughter. However, he was found guilty of being a felon in possession of a firearm. But even that conviction was overturned on a technicality by an appeals court.

During my career as an ICE agent, I encountered numerous people like Garcia-Zarate. Many had been arrested three or four times for committing crimes after entering the United States illegally. They had been convicted, served their time in prison, and been deported to their home countries. Then, as soon as possible, they made their way back across the border, committed another crime, and repeated the process. What can we do about these people? We can impose harsher sentences for second or third offenses so other illegal alien criminals can get the message that they had better stay out of our country. We can focus more on protecting American citizens than about protecting criminals from Mexico, Guatemala, Honduras and other countries around the world.

Sadly, the Steinle killing is not the only one that is blamed for misguided sanctuary city policies. In October of 2019, high school student Juan Carlos Guzman was murdered by two illegal aliens, one wielding a baseball bat and the other a machete. The victim was repeatedly beaten and hacked to death – with an arm and a leg being severed. Both of the men charged in the murder were members of the MS-13 gang. Apparently, King County authorities knew that the young men were in the country illegally, but failed to report them to ICE. After the crime, when ICE officials spoke about the connection between the killings and Sanctuary city policies, King County authorities accused ICE of harassing the county.

There have been a number of other murders and assaults in sanctuary cities around the country, and the fact is that they wouldn't have happened if ICE had been allowed to deal with these criminal undocumented aliens as the law, and common sense, dictate. For example, Luis Rodrigo Perez, an illegal alien from Mexico, was charged with killing two men and wounding two others in Missouri on November 1, 2018 and fatally shooting a woman the next day. He had been held on a domestic violence charge at the Middlesex County Jail in New Jersey before being released in February of 2018.

As was the case with the Seattle murders, ICE had lodged a detainer on Perez while he was in custody, but the request was not honored and ICE was not notified when he was released. Corey Price, acting executive associate director of ICE, said, "Yet again, an ICE detainer was ignored and a dangerous criminal alien was released to the streets and is now charged with killing three people." He added, "Had ICE's detainer request been honored by Middlesex County Jail, Luis Rodrigo Perez would have been placed in deportation proceedings and likely sent home to his country – and three innocent people might be alive today."[12]

Another high-profile murder case took place in California the day after Christmas last year when police officer Ronil Singh was gunned down in Stanislaus County. Singh, who was himself an immigrant, having come into the country legally from Fiji, was shot and killed after stopping Gustavo Perez Arriaga for suspected drunk driving. Singh left behind a wife and five-month-old son. According to ABC News, "At least three aliases were listed on Arriaga's criminal complaint, and authorities have said that he also used several different names on social media. Authorities also say that he has known gang affiliations."[13]

Stanislaus County Sheriff Adam Christianson blamed California's Sanctuary law for Singh's death, saying the law prevented the state from reporting Arriaga to ICE as "a criminal illegal alien."

The plain fact is that sanctuary cities are dangerous because the rights and safety of undocumented aliens seem to be valued more than the rights and safety of ordinary citizens. It is past time for mayors, city council members and other officials to realize that their first duty is to protect the people who live in their cities, and not the strangers who have come across our borders illegally. According to U.S. Immigration and Customs Enforcement estimates, there are roughly 2.1 million criminal aliens living in the United States. These criminal aliens continue to live in communities and engage in further criminal activity when state and local law enforcement are prohibited from cooperating with federal immigration officials.

In late 2019, in Fairfax County, Virginia, a police officer was sent to investigate a traffic accident. When he ran a check on the driver – which is standard procedure – he discovered that the man was an illegal and that ICE had an outstanding warrant that had

---

[12] conservativemedia.com/news, "Yet again an ICE detainer was ignored," accessed July 10, 2020

[13] abcnews.go.com/US, "Man suspected of killing California police officer Roni Singh charged with murder," accessed July 10, 2020

been issued after he failed to show up for a previous court hearing. The officer reported the man's arrest to the proper authorities. As a result, he was suspended from the police force for violating the sanctuary laws of Fairfax County. Thankfully, when the story got out, there was such an outcry that the officer was reinstated – as he should have been. This is yet another example of how crazy things can be in our sanctuary cities.

––––––––

Perhaps you've heard of the movement which goes by the name of Bail Reform. Proponents say that we need to do away with the practice of people paying bail to be released from jail. They say the system is unfair to poor people because they are less likely to be able to pay bail, and so they remain behind bars, while those with more money go free. Then again, paying bail isn't a way of buying your way out of jail. It's just a guarantee that if you are released you will come back and be in court on the day your case is heard. On the surface, doing away with bail sounds like a compassionate thing to do. But take a closer look, and you'll see that it makes it easier for everyone to get out of jail, including dangerous illegal alien criminals. As with so many other similar issues, it looks good on the surface, but there is more here than meets the eye. Many illegals remain in this country because they never showed up for their court date. Instead, they went into hiding, doing their best to blend into society. Bail reform will make it even easier to do this.

––––––––

Do you live in a sanctuary city? More importantly, would you like to know which sanctuary cities have the highest crime rates? Here is a top ten list (or should it be bottom ten?) that was recently compiled by the Immigration Reform Law Institute:[14]

---

[14] www.washingtonexaminer.com/washington-secrets/ Top 10 sanctuary cities with the highest crime

1. San Francisco
2. New York
3. Minneapolis
4. Philadelphia.
5. Seattle
6. Chicago
7. TIE: Montgomery County, Maryland, and Fairfax County, Virginia
8. Prince George's County, Maryland
9. Boston
10. Santa Clara County, California

If you see your city on this list, or even if you don't, it's important to raise your voice and let your elected officials know that you want to see the notion of sanctuary cities come to an end because you believe that illegal aliens who break the laws in this country should be deported. (By the way, research has shown that 80 percent of illegal immigrants who are released from jail after serving their sentences commit more crimes.)

Please understand that I am not saying that all undocumented aliens are criminals – even though it is true that they have broken our laws by sneaking into our country. But if they are already in jail for breaking other laws here in the United States, why should we turn them loose on our streets after they have served their time? Anyone who is here illegally and has shown himself to be a law-breaker should be sent back to their country of origin. It really is that simple.

In fact, one of the big issues we're facing as I write this book is the spread of the Coronavirus. To date, it has killed over 200,000 people here in the United States, and another half-million people around the world. I sincerely hope that by the time you are reading this book, we have developed a vaccine for this disease and it is under control.

By the way, if there is anything at all "good" about COVID-19, it's that it temporarily closed US borders. This closure at least stemmed the entry of illegal drugs from Mexico and gave rise to a sense of desperation within the cartels. While they are still manufacturing the drugs, they are struggling to get them into the United States. Supply is building up in Mexico, and there is a higher probability of detection. That is one small ray of light in a very dark situation.

But now we are hearing complaints from illegal aliens who are being held at ICE detention centers who say they are in danger from the Coronavirus because they are in close proximity to each other. They demand to be released so they will no longer be in danger. But what no one seems to talk about is that there is a simple answer to their predicament. If they don't want to be in detention, they can just ask to be sent back to their country of origin. Anyone who asks will be flown home, and it can happen as soon as tomorrow. They won't even have to walk for hundreds of miles, as they did on their journey north.

It seems to me that if they are truly afraid of the virus, they would gladly take our country's generous offer. But very few do. You see, they don't want to be released to go home. They want to be released into the United States – and that's strange because we are struggling with the virus, so they won't be any safer here.

It just goes to show that the illegal aliens will use any excuse they can find to gain access into the United States.

———

Now I want to take just a minute to talk about the importance of assimilation. Assimilation is a very important word that has fallen into disuse. I consider my mother and father prime examples of this, as they came to the United States from Mexico and assimilated into the culture. My dad doesn't fly the Mexican flag in front of his house. He flies the flag of the United States, and he's very proud of it. They did not move into a Mexican enclave and spend their lives clinging to customs and traditions they knew when they were children. While they are proud of their heritage, they consider themselves to be Americans now.

I've often heard it said that the United States is a country of immigrants. Yes, that's true, but we're a sovereign country. An older, more accurate term, is melting pot. In our history, legal immigrants from all over the world came here to become Americans and to assimilate into our western culture and our freedoms.

During the last several decades, many immigrants have come to the United States and created separate communities — smaller versions of their home countries — without assimilating. They segregate themselves from others. They want the best of both worlds. They want their country, their culture — everything except the bad things they left behind — here in the U.S. I believe that's a big problem in the long run, because they are separating themselves from the rest of the country and not creating a spirit of unity.

I mentioned that my dad flies the American flag in front of his house, but many immigrants fly their home country's flag. What are you saying if you're flying the flag from Mexico or some other country? You're saying you want the benefits, resources, and opportunities that the United States gives you, but you don't want to abide by the U.S. Constitution, laws and culture. That is divisive and not good for America.

To me, it's even more offensive if you're here illegally. You want to be here so badly, you risked everything you had to get here, and yet you won't assimilate.

I have one simple question. If you love your country so much, and if you hate the United States, then why are you living here?

I'm an American of Mexican descent. I love Mexican food and Mexican music, and I speak Spanish fluently. I don't have to deny my culture of origin—I can still enjoy my heritage. The American way of life is my way of life. In the city where I live, I am gratified to see people from many different cultures and countries living together in unity. That's the way it should be.

———

People often ask me what I think of the Deferred Action for Childhood Arrivals executive order that was signed by President Obama. This order provides certain protections for over 800,000 undocumented immigrants, who were brought to this country as children by their illegal alien parents. Most of them don't know what it's like to live in the countries they're from.

While my heart goes out to these young people, there are at least three issues.

First of all, something needs to be done legislatively to deal with this situation. An executive order is not sufficient. Congress needs to hammer out a law that spells out exactly how they will be treated.

Second, as a result of DACA, we've had an influx of illegal alien teenagers who now claim, wrongly, that they were brought here by their parents when they were younger. They're committing fraud and finding protection under DACA.

And it is also true, that some of those who _were_ brought to the United States as children have grown up to become gang members and criminals. These individuals do not deserve to be protected and given permanent residency in the United States. For that reason, we can't just offer blanket amnesty to all those who were brought here illegally when they were children. The Dreamers, as they're called, must be vetted and dealt with individually. No doubt, some of them should be considered to stay in the United States, but not all of them.

Chapter Thirteen
IMMIGRATION REFORM:
HOW TO REORGANIZE THE BROKEN SYSTEM

I llegal immigration is dangerous for everyone. Legal immigration, on the other hand, is generally a good thing.

These two things are far apart from each other. They are not the same at all. Unfortunately, liberals have comingled the two forms of immigration and talk about them as if they are the same. Immigrants are people who left their country of origin and came here legally. Illegals are those who chose not to go through the proper channels, and deliberately broke the law to get here.

We must not be fooled into thinking that illegal immigration is a good thing. It is not!

I have seen for myself how it destroys lives, not only here in the United States, but in Mexico, throughout Latin America, and in other countries where people are willing to risk their lives to get here. I have seen their bodies lying in the desert and I can only imagine the agony they felt in their last hours, when their throats were parched and dry, and the unrelenting sun beat down on them. I have been present when locked, abandoned truck trailers have been forced open, and the stench of death has poured out. What a terrible end for those who dreamed of a better life in America for themselves and their families.

Men, women, and children have all perished in the pursuit of the American dream. Some have been murdered. Some have been raped, beaten, and left for dead. The horrors of the human smuggling system that coyotes use are too numerous to mention. And yet, desperate people from Central and South American countries attempt the border crossing every day.

And, as we just saw in the last chapter, illegal immigration has terrible consequences for citizens of the United States. Kate Steinle would still be alive and well. So would Juan Carlos Guzman, Ronil Singh, and thousands of others. Right now, 40,000 criminal illegal and legal immigrants are incarcerated in federal prisons across the country, making up about 21 percent of the total federal prison population. According to Breitbart News, "Nearly all of those inmates are from Central and South America, resulting in a cost to U.S. taxpayers of about $1.4 billion every year."[15]

If you go online, you'll find some wild claims regarding how many Americans have been killed by undocumented immigrants. The last thing I ever want to do is exaggerate, because doing that hurts the push for immigration reform. But, let me tell you that Donald Trump was on target when he said "thousands of Americans have been killed" by illegal aliens. There are plenty of sad statistics to back that up. What can we do to stop this unnecessary suffering and dying? It's important to overhaul our country's immigration system. Here's how:

1) **The first step must be to properly enforce and strengthen our asylum system.** A new trend is now occurring. Illegal immigrants and criminals alike are coming into the U.S. in caravans, large groups of people requesting asylum. They are exploiting a loophole in our laws. The asylum system is supposed to be for people who are being persecuted, terrorized, or killed by their governments based on their race, nationality, religion, political opinion, or membership in a particular social group. The Syrian people, for example, are being gassed and terrorized by their government. This law is intended for that type of refugee. But now, since the Obama Administration changed the way the law is interpreted, illegal immigrants from Mexico and

---

[15] www.breitbart.com/politics/2018/08/17, "Nearly all criminal foreigners in the U.S. are from Central, South America, Accessed July 10, 2020

Central America are coming into the country as asylum seekers. In reality, they have no credible fear. Their lives are not in danger. They are not being persecuted based on their nationality or beliefs. They are coming to seek a better life for their families. They want to come here because we have a better economy. The asylum system makes it easy for them to circumvent the legal immigration system, which is time-consuming. Even worse, criminals are hiding in these large caravans, so they have an easy way into the United States.

When asylum seekers reach the border, their cases have to be processed. All children receive medical attention. Rape kits are provided to the women. And they are all fed and housed. The costs are astronomical. Asylum seekers are then provided with a court date for their hearing (to determine if they are allowed to remain in the U.S.). Right now, court dates are being scheduled two or three years into the future because the Department of Homeland Security is completely overwhelmed with the influx of people abusing the system. After that, asylum seekers are simply released, free to go wherever they want in the United States, never to be heard from again. In fact, over one million of them have deportation orders because they never showed up to their hearings.

2) **Streamline the process for legal immigrants.** The current U.S. legal immigration process is time-consuming and cumbersome. On average, it takes seven years to get approved to live and work in the Unites States. Why would migrants bother with this process when they are let into the country so easily as asylum seekers? In order to fix our illegal immigration problem, we need to change the protocols for both the asylum and immigration systems. We need to reward those immigrants who are trying to enter the country legally, who want to assimilate into our culture, and who want to contribute to our society. By the

way, despite the fact that the current process is cumbersome, according to the Migrant Policy Institute, in 2018 the United States allowed 1.1 million legal immigrants into the country. [16] The United States is a very generous country when it comes to legal immigration.

How can we streamline the process? One of the ways we can do this is by drastically reducing the processing times of those who want to come to the United States. As it now stands, the legal immigration process requires too many steps and applications have to be processed through too many government departments. For example, the requirements for medical exams, background checks, and other tests can be consolidated. I would love to see the creation of a one-stop shop or clinic, where a migrant can pay a fee and get all of these requirements done in one place. They could then submit their applications through an expedited system to *one* government department responsible for overseeing their approval. The idea is to discourage illegal immigration and encourage legal immigration. This would also naturally decrease the influx of criminals entering our country, as the improved communication channels would allow ICE to swiftly identify and remove criminals. Lastly, this plan would drastically cut costs, alleviating the pressures that American taxpayers now face due to the vulnerability of the asylum system. Yes, people who want to come into the United States must be thoroughly vetted – but there is no reason why the process can't be done faster.

3) **Get rid of "catch and release."** Catch and release is a capacity issue that pertains to asylum, unaccompanied minors and family units. When the Border Patrol catches an illegal alien, the date of his or her hearing is set – often months or even years down the line. He or she is then

---

[16] www,migrationpolicy.org, "Frequently Requested Statistics on Immigrants and Immigration," Accessed July 10, 2020

given a Notice to Appear and released into the United States to await the date of that hearing before a judge. We even bus them from border towns into the interior and drop them off. How many, do you suppose, return for their hearings? You're right. Very few.

I suggest that we change the system and make sure that those who have come into the country illegally are detained, and possibly prosecuted, and held until their court dates come up.

Another thing we can do to get rid of Catch and Release is to streamline and speed up the system. It shouldn't take a year or more for one of these cases to go before an immigration judge. The Department of Justice must hire additional Assistant U.S. Attorneys to manage new prosecutions.

It makes absolutely no sense to me that we are letting dangerous criminals go free on our streets. This is yet another case where the protection of the American people must take precedence over the "rights" of criminal illegal aliens. Along these same lines, I believe we must increase prosecution of illegal entry cases. Too many of those who sneak across our borders get away with what amounts to a slap on the wrist, and then wind up back in Mexico, where they launch their next "invasion" of the United States. Illegal entry into the United States is a crime and should be treated as such. We need more agents, prosecutors and judges to prosecute those who have been detained. For the sake of our country's well-being and safety, we must get serious about illegal immigration.

I would like to see the United States send the message that if you come across our border illegally, you will be caught, detained and serve time in jail, and then be sent back to your country of origin. It is time to protect the sovereignty of the United States. It comes down to a matter of national security.

4) **Overturn or amend the Flores Settlement.** Somehow, the interpretation of our asylum laws changed under the Obama administration. Migrants realized they could work the loopholes ... and there's a big loophole when it comes to the family unit. The Flores Settlement is not a law but a civil settlement made in 1993. This settlement states that those coming into the United States with a minor, or with a family unit, can only be placed in detention for a certain amount of time and then released.

Word soon spread. If you want to go start a new life in the United States, take your child with you and you'll be treated differently than if you go as an unaccompanied adult. In addition, if you come through Central America, you'll be treated differently than if you come from Mexico. As a result of this, caravans began forming in Central America, making their way north through Mexico. Stories of children being separated from their families and housed in cages elicited a huge uproar of disapproval from the American public. This practice began under the Obama Administration because of the wording of the Flores Settlement. These children are not placed in cages, but rather in temporary shelters, where they are protected from harm.

Because children cannot be housed with adults, they were, at one point, being held separately. It was then discovered that many of these children were *not* next of kin to the adults they were traveling with. In fact, determination to enter the United States through the "accompanied by a child" loophole led to additional child trafficking. Adults without children would arrange for any child to travel with them. In some instances, children have been "recycled" and have accompanied numerous so-called parents. We must send a message that these tactics will no longer work.

The Flores Settlement is still in effect, and with immigrants coming to our borders by the hundreds of thousands, we don't have the capacity or the facilities available to detain them. Migrants are released with instructions to return for asylum hearings when they receive notification in the mail. Unfortunately, the backlog is so great that the hearings are sometimes scheduled for two or three years later, and the migrants never return.

5) **Make it a priority to deport criminal aliens from the United States.** There are some really dangerous people walking the streets of America – people who pledge their allegiance to gangs like MS13 and Barrio Azteca. You will remember the story about Juan Carlos Guzman, a high school student who was bludgeoned and slashed to death by two members of MS13. Those savages never should have been in this country. It is high time we declare war on these organizations and sweep them out of the United States.

6) **Send people home when their visas expire.** As it currently stands, thousands of people come into this country on tourist visas, and then just stay here. The United States does virtually nothing to find them and send them home. Now, it's true that people who come here on a visa are probably better off than those who sneak across the broiling desert to reach our borders. That's no reason to show them preference. They are in the United States illegally, just the same as those who wade across the Rio Grande or are brought into the United States in trucks driven by coyotes. All illegal aliens should be held accountable under our law.

Remember that the 19 hijackers who attacked our country on 9/11 came here on visas and then killed 3,000 Americans. I don't want to have another attack like that, and I'm sure you don't either. It's time to vet and overhaul our visa program, and to take control of our borders and protect our sovereignty.

7) **Prosecute juvenile drug smugglers.** The cartels love to find teenagers to carry drugs into the United States for them. I mentioned before that I've seen these youth carry backpacks full of pot and other drugs across the border and leave them in the desert for someone else to pick up. Some of these teens are from Mexico, but others are American citizens. They may be held for a few hours, but then they're released, and are back at work in a day or two. Some of them have been across the border dozens of times – perhaps even hundreds of times, and I, for one, think it's absurd that we let them get away with it. I'm not suggesting we should throw them in jail for life, but we ought to at least do something that will make them think long and hard about doing it again. In many cases, a 16-year-old who commits a major crime is charged as an adult. I believe we must do the same thing with these young smugglers at the federal level. Right now, they are breaking our laws with impunity, and this must be stopped. No one wants to put these teens in jail, but those who are running drugs for the Mexican cartels left their childhoods behind a long time ago.

The teenagers who work for the cartels don't usually bring a lot of drugs into this country at one time – but they cross the border so many times and it all adds up. For instance, I once arrested a young guy – he was 19 or 20, so old enough to prosecute – who had brought 250 pounds of marijuana into the country. In the course of questioning him, I asked him how many times he had smuggled drugs across the border.

"Maybe ten," he replied.

"Ten times? Are you sure?

He nodded. "Yeah, ten times."

166

His defense attorney was livid when I charged him with smuggling 2,500 pounds of pot into the United States (250 x 10). The amount was reduced slightly by the judge, but the suspect was still convicted of smuggling more than 250 pounds into the country and he got a stiffer sentence. That's the kind of thing we need to do to stop the flow of drugs into this country. We must make it harder for smugglers, not easier.

8) **Do away with thresholds that hamper prosecution of drug smugglers and human smugglers.** What do I mean by thresholds? In some instances, a couple of pounds of drugs can make the difference between a federal and local charge which can make a substantial difference in a smuggler's prison sentence. The same is true of those who are smuggling illegal aliens into the country. A certain number of aliens brings federal charges and longer prison sentences. I believe that penalties should be harsh for anyone who breeches our border security, no matter how many drugs or illegal aliens they have with them. I may sound hard-nosed, but I'm convinced that's what it's going to take to reduce the amount of drugs and illegals coming into this country.

9) **Hold Mexico Accountable.** The United States has poured billions of dollars into Mexico to help with security issues there and, frankly, we haven't seen much in the way of results. We must hold the Mexican government accountable, and work with them to beef up their own internal security. A more secure Mexico means a more secure United States. For instance, a few years ago, I was involved in conducting an assessment of Mexico's southern border, along with Mexican Immigration, Customs and the Mexican Navy. I discovered that there is practically no security at all between Mexico and Guatemala. People were walking back and forth across the border like it didn't even exist. Children were actually running from

one country to the other to sell fruit and flowers. Anyone who wanted to cross the border and get one step closer to the United States could do so – without question. An open border between Mexico and Guatemala only makes the U.S. border less secure.

10) **Hire additional Border Patrol Agents, Border Protection Officers, and Homeland Security Special Agents** to help stop the flow of illegal immigration and drugs into the United States. I also believe we should shift our existing resources to our southern border to create a "surge of enforcement." A surge of American troops helped us vanquish our foes in Iraq, and a surge of law enforcement personnel along our border will help keep criminals out of our country. We could improve border security by bringing all the agents from the interior of the country to the Southwestern border for a period of 12 to 18 months.

I admit that some liberal groups, such as the ACLU, would be very upset if we did something like this. But remember what I said before about the vast difference between legal and illegal immigration. We can't allow the two to become comingled in our minds or our national policies. We must toughen our stand against illegal immigration.

11) **Expand investigations of Special Interest Aliens (SIA's),** especially those that are in Mexico or want to come through Mexico to get into the U.S. Unfortunately, there are a lot of people out there who hate the United States and want to get into this country to do us harm. It's important to do a a better job of identifying these individuals and closing our borders to them. In June of 2019, an ISIS plan to send English-speaking terrorists into the United States was uncovered when one of the recruits backed out and exposed the mission. Previously, Arab terrorists were stopped before they could smuggle anthrax into the United States. And in Edmonton, Canada,

recently, Abdulahi Hasan Sharif was found guilty on five counts of attempted murder. Sharif, from Somalia, had been arrested after illegally coming into the United States from Mexico, and the judge ordered him to be deported back to Africa. Instead, Sharif made his way to Edmonton. There, he rented a U-Haul truck and led police on a chase, during which he slammed into four pedestrians. Prior to renting the U-Haul vehicle, he used his own car to run-down police officer Mick Chernyk, and then jumped out and stabbed the victim in the head. Miraculously all of Sharif's victims survived. Not surprisingly, the Somali native had an ISIS flag in his vehicle when he was arrested. This violent rampage, or worse, could have happened in the United States.

12) **Stop programs like MEDPAR**, which is an entitlement program that provides medical care for illegal aliens. It's one thing to allow illegal aliens into our country, but it's quite another to provide them with free medical services, education and other entitlements. It creates a terrible burden on American taxpayers, and it strikes me as grossly unfair that illegals should get for free what so many American citizens struggle for. Currently, we're experiencing a spike of COVID-19, especially in the southwestern United States, as sick people are coming from Mexico and are being admitted into U.S. hospitals. They are taking up valuable hospital beds and ICU space. Some border towns have even experienced maximum capacity and are transporting illegals into interior hospitals to get treated. I don't want anyone anywhere to suffer and die from COVID-19, but I also believe that American citizens must be our first priority. No American citizen should be turned away in order that a person from Mexico – or any other country – can be treated.

Chapter Fourteen

WHAT YOU CAN DO TO HELP

I hope that by now I've made my point that it's important for the United States to strengthen the security along our Southern border. I also hope that you want to get involved in changing our immigration policy and border security. You can. Here's how:

First of all, I hope you will do further research on the topics we've discussed in this book. I urge you to avoid the myths that are often circulated by both political parties on social media. I believe it's dangerous to get all of your information about a political topic from one source, whether that source is social media, the internet, or the main-stream media. All media outlets are biased in one way or another. In addition, many of them get the facts wrong. After Jaime and I were ambushed by the Los Zetas cartel, I read in some news reports that the names of the victims were Jaime Avila and Victor Zapata, creating confusion as to which of us had survived the shooting. Unfortunately, news stations often fail to do their fact-checking. That's just one of the reasons why I think it's important for readers to try to hear all sides of a story and to get accurate information on a topic before having a knee-jerk reaction. Too many people allow others to do their thinking for them. If we are going to change policy, we first need to step up and think for ourselves.

Second, be wary of believing and sharing social media posts, which are often inaccurate and inflammatory. Popular social media posts often play off viewers emotions in order to promote a particular political point of view. They are usually misleading. Instead,

I encourage you to question these kinds of posts and to use social media to create awareness about important social issues.

Third, it's important that you get to know local officials and reach out to them about topics of interest, that you vote on important issues, and let your friends and other associates know how you feel. If you don't already know, learn who represents you in the government at the local, state and federal level. The United States government—at any level—is designed to work for the people. These elected officials represent us, and in order to do that, they need to hear how we feel about our issues. Yes, you can contact them, and I urge you to do just that. Make your voice heard and relay your concerns.

If you can, attend city council and county meetings, where citizens like you and me are given an opportunity to express ourselves on various topics. It's also important to stay informed about new bills that are being proposed in your state legislature. Many bills are proposed at the state level every month, and if these bills are passed, they are made into laws that can directly impact us.

And lastly, I hope you will create awareness about immigration policies and border security issues whenever possible. Bring up these topics in friendly conversation. Talk to your youth, so they are informed and don't become victims themselves. And provide your social circles with informative website links, elected officials' phone numbers, or other relevant resources.

As Thomas Jefferson said, "Whenever the people are well-informed, they can be trusted with their own government."

As I write these final words, our country is in turmoil. The tragic death of George Floyd, who died at the hands of Minneapolis police, has stirred nationwide protests of an unprecedented scale. At first, protesters were proclaiming that Black Lives Matter, and standing against racial injustice. I support peaceful assembly as our constitutional right. All lives matter! And, of course, we must be willing to stamp out racism whenever and wherever we find it.

However, what started off as peaceful protests quickly became rioting, looting, destruction of property and the murder of police officers. It seemed to me that the protests became more anti-police than anti-racism.

However, I don't believe there is systemic racism in our country or in our police forces. Almost all of the law enforcement officers I have known and worked with are upstanding people who honestly serve and protect. During my time in ICE, I never heard any of my colleagues use derogatory language about people of another race or ethnicity. I have never met anyone wearing a uniform who I thought was a racist. Yes, there probably are racist officers, and we need to weed them out. But we cannot condemn all law enforcement because of those few.

You can be against racism and still support the police at the same time. Are there bad cops? Of course, just as there are bad lawyers, bad teachers, bad plumbers, etc. There are good and bad people in every walk of life. Wouldn't it be wonderful if everyone obeyed the law, treated other people fairly and with respect, and there was no need for law enforcement. But that's not the world we live in.

There is only one way to fight hatred, racism, crime and violence – and that is together!

For the sake of our country, it's time do what we did after the attacks of 9/11. We must put our differences aside and move forward in a spirit of cooperation and unity. America's future depends on it.

EPILOGUE

J ust as this book was about to go to press, some important
events took place. One of these, which brought me a measure
of vindication after all these years, was that the U.S. Office of
Special Counsel completed its investigation into the events sur-
rounding the assignment that led to Jaime and me being attacked
on Highway 57.

Special Counsel Henry J. Kerner, who helped lead the investigation said, "Agents Avila and Zapata were put in harm's way
while serving their country, without adequate support. We owe it
to those who continue to put their lives on the line to ensure our
agents have the resources they need when assigned to dangerous
missions."

The investigation, which was conducted by the ICE Office of
Professional Responsibility found gross mismanagement in our
office. ICE officials failed to provide Jaime and me with additional
support for our mission from either U.S. personnel or Mexican law
enforcement. Investigators also concluded that the agency failed
to properly brief and prepare us in advance of the assignment to
discuss the cargo, security measures, and any other relevant information – and referred to "a known lack of diligence with regard
to the maintenance of the ICE armored vehicles."

According to a press release issued by the U.S. Office of
Special Counsel:

"The investigation revealed that, at the time of the attack, management lacked specific policies and procedures for the execution
of the agency mission in Mexico. For example, the agency lacked
formalized policies with respect to travel; did not provide counter

threat training to those stationed in Mexico; and did not provide armored vehicle training to employees in Mexico. Additionally, the Mexico City office suffered from weak operational security, which was evident in the lack of planning and execution for the trip taken by Agent Avila and Agent Zapata."

I also received the following letter from the U.S. Office of Special Counsel, which is printed in its entirety:

> *Dear Mr. Avila:*
>
> *The U.S. Office of Special Counsel (OSC) has completed its review of the report of an internal investigation by U.S. Immigration and Customs Enforcement (ICE) into your disclosures. You alleged that in February 2011, officials at the ICE Office of the Attaché in Mexico City engaged in gross mismanagement when they sent you and Special Agent Jaime Zapata on an assignment that required you to travel near areas controlled or monitored by members of Los Zetas drug cartel, without taking necessary steps in advance of the assignment. Cartel members attacked you during the trip, killing Agent Zapata and wounding you.*
>
> *The agency investigation substantiated the allegations that ICE-HSI officials failed to consider the possibility of, or improperly declined to provide or coordinate, additional support with U.S. personnel and/or Mexican law enforcement; failed to coordinate with the relevant Regional Security Officer for the trip; and failed to properly brief and prepare you in advance of the assignment to discuss the cargo, security measures, and any other relevant information. The report also confirmed other problems and issues, including with respect to faulty equipment, lack of specific policies and procedures, weak operational security, and complacency toward the dangers of travel in Mexico.*

As the report noted, since this tragic event occurred, ICE and HSI implemented several reforms. ICE also indicated that the report would be forwarded to HSI Executive Leadership for consideration of disciplinary action.

Today, the Special Counsel forwarded to the President the agency report based on the disclosures you filed with our office. A copy of the letter is enclosed. As stated in the letter, the Special Counsel determined that the ICE report meets statutory requirements, and the findings appear reasonable.

As required by 5 U.S.C. § 1213(e)(3), OSC has also sent copies of its determination and the agency report to the Chairmen and Ranking Members of the Senate Committee on Homeland Security and Governmental Affairs and the House Committee on Homeland Security. OSC has also filed redacted copies of these documents and the redacted section 1213 referral in our public file, which is available at www.osc.gov. If you would like to disseminate the report, please use the publicly available redacted version.

Thank you for bringing this matter to our attention. If you have any questions or concerns, please contact me at CLeo@osc.gov or (202) 804-7074. This matter is now closed.

Sincerely
Christopher Leo Attorney Retaliation and Disclosure Unit

Included in the materials sent to me was the following letter from Henry J. Kerner to *President Donald Trump:*

177

Dear Mr. President:
Pursuant to my duties as Special Counsel, I am forwarding to you a report provided to me in response to disclosures received from former Special Agent Victor Avila of the Department of Homeland Security (DHS), Immigration and Customs Enforcement (ICE), Homeland Security Investigations (HSI). Agent Avila, who consented to the release of his name, alleged that in February 2011, officials at the ICE Office of the Attaché in Mexico City engaged in gross mismanagement when they sent him and Special Agent Jaime Zapata, who was on temporary duty assignment (TDY) to Mexico City at the time, on a dangerous assignment through areas controlled or monitored by Los Zetas drug cartel. ICE-HSI Mexico City management tasked the two agents with traveling north to an area near the city of Matehuala, Mexico to meet with ICE agents from the ICE-HSI office in Monterrey, Mexico to obtain equipment. During the return trip to Mexico City after the meeting, cartel members attacked them, killing Agent Zapata and wounding Agent Avila.

Agent Avila alleged that ICE-HSI officials: (1) ignored advisories from the U.S. Department of State (DOS), Diplomatic Security Service, regarding travel dangers along the route to the meeting point; (2) ignored intelligence indicating travel dangers along the route to the meeting point; (3) failed to consider the possibility of, or improperly declined to provide or coordinate, additional support for the agents with U.S. personnel and/ or Mexican law enforcement; (4) failed to coordinate with the relevant Regional Security Officer (RSO) for the trip; 2 (5) failed to consider the possibility of using, or improperly declined the use of, a diplomatic pouch to transport the cargo via ground or air; and (6) failed to properly brief and prepare the agents in advance of the assignment to discuss the cargo, security measures, and any other relevant information.

The investigation substantiated the allegations that ICE-HSI officials failed to consider the possibility of, or improperly declined to provide or coordinate, additional support for the agents with U.S. personnel and/or Mexican law enforcement; failed to coordinate with the relevant RSO for the trip; and failed to properly brief and prepare the agents in advance of the assignment to discuss the cargo, security measures, and any other relevant information. Additionally, the report confirmed that there was "a known lack of diligence with regard to the maintenance of the ICE armored vehicles." For example, it was known in the ICE-HSI Mexico City office prior to the incident that the agents' armored vehicle did not have properly functioning tracking equipment.

The investigation also found that, at the time of the attack, management lacked specific policies and procedures for the execution of the agency mission in Mexico. For example, the agency lacked formalized policies with respect to travel; did not provide counter threat training to those stationed in Mexico (except for those working along the border who received such training from DOS); and did not provide armored vehicle training to employees in Mexico. Additionally, the Mexico City office suffered from weak operational security, which was evident in the lack of planning and execution for the trip taken by Agent Avila and Agent Zapata.

The report did not substantiate the allegation that officials failed to consider the possibility of using, or improperly declined the use of, a diplomatic pouch to transport the cargo via ground or air. The report notes that use of a pouch was discussed but was determined to take too long. Furthermore, the report does not substantiate the two allegations that officials ignored DOS advisories and intelligence about the travel dangers but does acknowledge managerial complacency toward the dangers of traveling in Mexico.

The report confirms that, in the aftermath of the relevant events, ICE addressed this mismanagement by (1) establishing a Personnel Recovery Unit to "provid[e] ICE employees and their families with the knowledge and capabilities to prepare for, prevent, respond to, and survive an isolating event while deployed overseas"; (2) implementing restrictions on driving in Mexico, "to include no self-driving outside of city limits" and requiring "a minimum of two people and 24-hour notice to the RSO"; (3) increasing training for all personnel assigned to Mexico, including Foreign Affairs Counter Threat training; (4) mandating that all personnel complete High Threat Security Overseas prior to deployment to Mexico on TDY; (5) mandating armored vehicle training for all personnel in Mexico; and (6) disabling the automatic unlocking mechanism in HSI armored vehicles. Additionally, the report was forwarded to HSI Executive Leadership to consider disciplinary action.

I am saddened not only by the significant harm to Agent Avila, but the death of Agent Zapata as well. I am grateful to Agent Avila for notifying my office of his concerns about the potential mismanagement immediately preceding this tragic event and for allowing us the opportunity to seek answers to his concerns. While what happened to Agent Avila is terrible, I am pleased to see that the agency has taken steps to help prevent such a tragedy from occurring in the future.

I have reviewed the original disclosure and the agency report. Agent Avila also reviewed the agency report and provided his own comments to OSC, but prefers to keep those comments confidential. Based on the substantiation of three of the referred allegations, inclusion of other instances of mismanagement not specifically identified in our referral, and in consideration of the actions taken by the agency to address these problems, I have determined that the report contains the information required by statute, and the findings appear reasonable.

As required by 5 U.S.C. § 1213(e)(3), I have sent copies of this letter and the agency report to the Chairmen and Ranking Members of the Senate Committee on Homeland Security and Governmental Affairs and the House Committee on Homeland Security. I have also filed redacted copies of these documents and a redacted copy of the referral letter in our public file, which is available online at www.osc.gov, and closed the matter.

Respectfully,
Henry J. Kerner
Special Counsel

CPSIA information can be obtained
at www.ICGtesting.com
Printed in the USA
LVHW071955031120
670479LV00005BA/129